Sips of Sustenance

Grieving the loss of your spouse

With words of wisdom from great writers

Sherry L. Hoppe, Ed.D.

WAKESTONE PRESS

Nashville, Tennessee

Sips of Sustenance
Grieving the loss of your spouse
by Sherry L. Hoppe

Copyright © 2010 by Sherry L. Hoppe

Wakestone Press, L.L.C.
200 Brook Hollow Road
Nashville, Tennessee 37205

http://www.wakestonepress.com

ISBN: 978-1-60956-007-2

Library of Congress Control Number: 2011926054

Dedicated to the memory of

Bob Hoppe,

Whose love dwells within me

Whose spirit sustains me still

In this sad world of ours, sorrow comes to all,
and it often comes with bitter agony.
Perfect relief is not possible,
except with time.
You cannot believe that you will ever feel better.
But this is not true.
You are sure to be happy again.
Knowing this,
truly believing it,
will make you less miserable now.
I have had enough experience to make this statement.

--Abraham Lincoln

Table of Contents

Introduction

Did someone say that there would be an end,
An end,
Oh, an end to love and mourning?

--May Sarton

The agony of losing a spouse sparks such a searing fire in our soul we can hardly breathe. Surely, we think, no one has ever felt such depths of despair. Smothering in sorrow, the future so black we cannot visualize it, we struggle with how to survive a moment at a time. When others offer sympathy and counsel, we cringe, not wanting to listen. In our rebellion, words of wisdom must come in small doses, as sips of sustenance to nourish our grieving spirit.

Death almost always arrives as an unwelcome visitor. Having watched both parents die excruciatingly slow deaths from painful terminal illnesses, I once thought losing a loved one quickly would be a blessing. Years later, when I found my husband lying dead on the kitchen floor with no forewarning, I realized there is no good way to lose anyone who is dearly loved. Whether death announces its imminent summons, warning us of its approach, or sneaks into our lives like a tiger in the jungle, pouncing suddenly and unexpectedly, the harsh reality of loss can send even the strongest person spiraling into a lightless shaft.

Crawling out of the chasm of loss may seem impossible, and for a time we may not want to try. After all, if we remain buried in our sorrow, we delay returning to the world of the living. We can pretend it's all a bad dream—that we will wake up and find death never called. But as surely as the coming of a full moon, eventually we must pull ourselves out of the abyss to face life without our loved one.

Death is not negotiable after it arrives on our doorstep. As much as we would like to turn back the clock and return our beloved to the physical world, it will not happen. Young or old, we must continue the journey of life without our husband or wife by our side. The question is how to do that; and, although no magical answer exists, many great writers have wisdom to share. This book is built on their words of insight.

As individuals, we can learn from others' thoughts and experiences, but we have to find our own way through grief to the other side. No arbitrary timetable can be established for the progression—the suffering moves at its own pace for each person. We may never get over our loss, but we can get through the grieving process.

Introduction

Although I write from the experience of my own loss, I would not presume to compare it to yours. Just as the person you loved was unique, so shall be your grieving. This book is thus not a roadmap to healing — it simply offers a few signposts from well-known authors, as well as a few lesser-known writers, to help point you in the right direction when you feel immobilized by your loss.

While there is some logical flow of topics in the book, it doesn't have to be read from start to finish — just flip through the pages or scan the contents section and choose the topic that meets your need on any particular day. If you are grieving, you have a rough journey ahead, and this book may supply light along the way. Hope that how you feel today — that the depth and breadth of the grief that has thrown you into the bottomless pit — will diminish. And perhaps, even though it is hard to envision now, on a far horizon, an end to the deep mourning. The possibility that — though it will be different — you will someday find a way to enjoy life again.

Sips of Sustenance

Chapter 1

The First Few Days

Faith is not simply a patience that passively suffers until the storm is past. Rather, it is a spirit that bears things – with resignation, yes, but above all, with blazing, serene hope.

--Corazon Aquino

How can the loss of a dearly loved spouse be described? Are there words to express how we feel? The sickness in the pit of our stomach, the shocked realization our husband or wife is gone, never to return, the panic that he or she won't be there for us. Profound sadness. Numbness. Desolation. Apprehension. Fear. Words sound so mundane compared to the breadth and depth of our emotions. If we can't even express our grief, how can we get through the days ahead?

If death of the person with whom we hoped to spend the rest of our lives caught us unaware, disbelief may have stunned us into silence. Like the stillness before a summer storm, our whole being may have paused before tears were finally unleashed, leaving us helpless, unable to slow the raging squall. For others, tears may come more quickly, rushing forth in torrents from the moment of death. Whether immediate or delayed, we wonder if the crying will ever cease.

Sips of Sustenance

If death came on the wings of suffering, the first reaction may have been relief; relief our loved one was no longer in pain. But likely any respite soon gave way to sadness, and tears flowed, drowning our soul. As Voltaire knew, "Tears are the silent language of grief." Even when we are too sorrowful to speak words, tears convey our anguish.

Grief counselors advise us not to hold back tears, taking their cue from writers like Shakespeare, who held that "To weep is to make less the grief." And, for a while, tears helped, supplying a safety valve to release pressure from the heavy burden placed on our heart.

When we could cry no more, we turned to the busyness of preparing for the service that memorialized our loved one's life. There was much to be done in a short time, and we were glad to have something to do. Decisions had to be managed; details handled, and selections made. Someone was always at our side, guiding, helping, comforting us as we completed the requisite tasks.

Somehow we got through the service and then turned to the business of ending our spouse's physical life. Wills had to be found, read, and probated. Insurance matters required attention. Money matters had to be reviewed. And, now or later, personal possessions must be touched with loving hands and decisions made about their disposition. Still, a friend or relative stayed by us.

The First Few Days

And then everyone goes back to his or her life—the ones they are living with their loved ones who are still in this world—and we are alone with our grief.

At first, we may just sit and stare into space for hours on end. Tears may flow unbidden, sometimes quietly and sometimes a tidal wave sucking us under. At other times we sit dry-eyed, unable to cry any more. We feel immobilized, without the strength or the will to move.

Alone, anger may erupt, and we shriek at our husband or wife for leaving us alone. We may rail at God, accusing him of robbing us prematurely. It's not fair. In the shower, head bowed under a cascade of water, screams echo our grief.

So how do we get through the initial moments of despair, days when grief threatens to overwhelm us?

First, let the grief flow—in whatever way it comes. Don't try to hold back the sadness, the anger, the fear, the helplessness. Moliere advised our grief "can well redouble" if we suppress it too much. In simpler words, sorrow becomes a pressure cooker waiting to explode if steam isn't allowed to escape. We will find, in Ovid's words, "It is some relief to weep; grief is satisfied and carried off by tears."

Second, it's okay to stand still for a while. Although others may be going about the routines of their lives, our life has stopped in its tracks, a train with no steam to run its engine. Logic, reasoning, encouragement, cajoling, threats—all go unheard when friends and family try to lift us from the pit into which we have fallen.

We should do only what we feel like doing when we feel like doing it. When well-meaning friends and family insist we join them in activities, they can be asked to respect our need to be alone. Staring into space may bother others, but it insulates us from thinking unbearable thoughts. When we need to come up for air — to become more active or spend time with others — we will know it. Still, in the midst of the storm, we should endeavor to never lose hope. We must try to remember not just our loss, but what we had. For, as Vincent van Gogh said, "The fishermen know that the sea is dangerous and the storm terrible, but they have never found these dangers sufficient reason for remaining ashore." Similarly, despite the storm in our souls, we would never have wanted to stay ashore and miss the journey we had with our soul mate.

If we listen, the storm may have a message for us. We should remember, as Willa Cather avowed, "There are some things you learn best in calm and some in storm."

The First Few Days

Today I will be thankful for the support of family and friends, but I realize they must return to their own lives. In the moments after they move on, and the busyness of ending life concludes, I will do what my body and soul tell me I need to do—nothing more and nothing less. And I will listen for what the storm has to tell me.

Chapter 2

Why?

Pale Death with impartial tread beats at the poor man's cottage door and at the palaces of kings.

--Horace

After death stalks through the door, one of the hardest questions—and one we ask repeatedly—begins with a single word: Why?

Why my loved one? Why now? Why in this way? Why? Why? Why?

The "why's" ring—a gong struck with a mallet. At first the sound screams at us, before fading into quiet reverberations—until the hammer hits again and the sound ricochets back into the air in full velocity before drifting away once more. Over and over again the "why's" resound, and no answers come. Just a three-letter word haunting us in countless ways.

As Horace said, death is impartial. It does not discriminate. It comes to the door of the rich and to the door of the poor. To those just beginning their lives together. To those settling in to their middle years. To those in their twilight years.

Death cares not. It swoops into our lives, a hungry hawk carrying off the person we cherish. At our most uncharitable moment, we wish it were someone else's beloved. Anyone. Just not the person who made our life whole.

We howl at the heavens because the time is not right. There was so much more to be done in our spouse's life. So many more times to be shared. But in our heart, we know there would never be a time we would be ready to give up our loved one. There would be no convenient time for death to intrude. We would never be ready to say goodbye, mindful of the clever question in *The Music Man*: "Where is the *good* in goodbye?"

As Queen Elizabeth I said, we would give "All of [our] possessions for a moment of time." We would like to bargain. Just a little more time. If we could just keep our husband or wife on earth for a month, a week, or even a day, we would willingly offer all our prized belongings.

Why couldn't we have had more time together? Why didn't we do more things when we had the chance? But in the midst of our questions, Mason Cooley strikes a warning: "Regret for wasted time is more time wasted."

Somerset Maugham instructed us not to think of the past—all that matters, he said, is "the everlasting present." A present that no longer includes our loved one. A present made bleak by his or her absence. It's hard to let go of the past. Impossible not to think of what could have been.

In the depths of despair, we may even wish it had been we who died. Why could we not have been the one taken? Or why could death have not invited both of us to go side by side on its voyage?

On and on go the "why's," replicated in a thousand different ways. How do we stop the simple yet heart-wrenching questions? Our thoughts are disjointed, lapsing into a blur at times, but the three-letter word stays etched in our minds. Time moves slowly—too slowly, and we are reminded of Henry Van Dyke's words: "Time is too slow for those who wait, too swift for those who fear, too long for those who grieve, too short for those who rejoice, but for those who love, time is eternity."

Too slow for those who grieve but eternity for those who love. Two incompatible phrases. In our grief, we mourn for the love we wanted to last forever, wanting responses to "why."

In the end, we will probably not find answers. But, if we are willing to suspend rational thought, we can get beyond the "why's" and hold on to what we can. After all, what is love? It's not a tangible object we can clutch in our hands. Is it possible it did not die with our spouse? Can we not carry the love we shared in our heart, where it resided when our loved one was at our side? If we but think differently, we can hold on to what we treasured even if we have unanswered questions.

Why?

In the midst of my questions,

I will still the reverberations

and hold close the love that still

survives in my heart.

Chapter 3

Pain

There is no coming to consciousness without pain.
--Carl Jung

There is no pain like grief. The aching for the other person's presence is so intense we have trouble describing it in words. It wouldn't do any good if we could. Each loss is unique, because the person who vanished from our lives was made from a distinctive mold. Our connection to that person is akin to no other connection between two people. No one else can get inside our sorrow with us, because they were not part of that private bond. No one else can understand our pain. No one else feels the absence as we do.

The hurt emanates from the love we lost. And yet, as C.S. Lewis noted, "The pain now is part of the happiness then. That's the deal."

If we accept love, we have to be willing to accept the pain of loss. The only way to diminish the sting is to deny the love, and we surely don't want to go down that path.

So our heart throbs with pain over the broken link with the person we loved. Part of our world has died, and what's left is no longer satisfying. Without our spouse at our side, can we ever find joy in life again? How do we get through the agony?

For some, isolation is the temporary answer. Alone, we can dwell on our grief, absorbing the suffering as we sit mindless, staring at a blank future. The physical isolation from our beloved is intense. We were close, and now that person is no longer at our side. We walked together, shopped together, played together, ate together. Now, we do all those things alone. And the ache of the absence grips us, enveloping us in its claws, an eagle clutching its prey.

Friends ask, why don't you try to do something? Go out for a while with us? For some, this may help, but only we can decide what works for us along the grief journey. If we step out prematurely, we may find ourselves knocked back by even more pain.

In our sorrow, whether we isolate ourselves or walk among friends and family like the shadow of the person we once were, we need to be careful that hope doesn't disappear. Even in despair, no longer able to see life beyond the prison in which we find ourselves, we need to propel ourselves outside the invisible walls keeping us locked in our pain. Some do this physically by joining grief groups or just being in the midst of others for support; others escape with music; still others seek solace in meditation. Many find comfort in nature.

Pain

The ways are as different as we are, but we all need to find antidotes.

We must occasionally anesthetize ourselves, numbing the tender areas to give temporary reprieves from hurting so badly we think we cannot endure. We may not be able to escape pain, but we can briefly suppress it to a different level of our consciousness. We must go through the anguish of loss to return to living, but we don't have to dwell there every waking moment.

If we are fortunate, as Pierre-Auguste Renoir said, "The pain passes, but the beauty remains." Coming to a conscious acceptance of our pain is the first step in coming to an acceptance of our loss. "Pain and death are a part of life," Havelock Ellis told us, and "to reject pain is to reject life itself."

For a few moments today, I will

relegate pain to another realm of my

consciousness while I find breathing

space.

Chapter 4

Living with Regrets

Waste not fresh tears over old griefs.

--Euripides

Whether death crept in softly, in Sandburg's words, "on little cat paws," or stomped in the front door, unannounced, most of us have regrets. Thoughts spin in our heads like the vortex of a tornado: I should have been kinder. I uttered such hateful words at her. I did not spend enough time with him. I didn't say "I love you" often enough. The last words I said were hurled in anger. We should have traveled while we had the chance. We could have waited to make the trip.

Each person's list is different, but we all have a list. Everyone has regrets. And they hurt. They force themselves unbidden into our minds and twist, daggers in our heart. We try to still them, but they won't be silenced.

Sometimes the regrets come as *if only's*: If only I hadn't let him leave alone...if only I had stayed home...if only I had been there...if only I hadn't made her mad...if only I had forced him see a doctor.... We can all substitute our own *if only's*.

Sips of Sustenance

We torture ourselves with regrets and *what if*s, scourging ourselves unmercifully. Guilt and blame engulf us, causing suffering deeper than the grief of loss itself. Sophocles was right: "The greatest griefs are those we cause ourselves." Death has a merciless way of making us helpless, because we know we can't change what we did or didn't do. The regrets magnify in our minds, and no matter how we deal with them intellectually, we can't erase them from our hearts.

Because I was emotionally distant from my husband in the two weeks before his unexpected death, I couldn't forgive myself. The raging guilt was so strong, I even calculated what percent two weeks were of our 37 years together—less than one-tenth of one percent. Too much, I chastised myself. No matter how much I tried to convince myself I had been there emotionally for my beloved 99.9 percent of our time together, I couldn't do it. Resembling a recording caught in a continuous loop, repeating the same phrase over and over, I played the "if only" song in my head.

I tried to convince myself he hadn't noticed. But I think he had. I told myself those two weeks no longer mattered to him. It didn't help. I just kept beating myself up.

At some point, months later, the realization dawned on me that I had to forgive myself. I had to adopt Reinhold Niebuhr's serenity prayer: "God grant me the serenity to accept the things I cannot change, the courage to change the things I can, and the wisdom to know the difference." At first, the words could only shut out the regret for a moment, but now, even though regret returns unbidden sometimes, it does not occupy my mind every waking moment.

We choose what we think, and sometimes we choose to think of our regrets; but sometimes we can make a conscious choice not to think about them. To replace them with happier memories—a walk on the beach together, a stroll in a summer shower, the sighting of a scarlet cardinal in all its splendor, an exchange of loving glances—after all, isn't that how our loved ones would want us to remember them?

We can gather the memories of the journey we traveled together, the moments shared, the times that made us smile—or weep: the majesty of a sunset on the rim of the horizon, the wordless looks that spoke of love, the silent touch of caring, the joyous first snowfall of the winter. These memories should not be veiled in regret. They are what we were and still are. They did not die with our loved one. They remain to comfort us. If we won't silence them, they will speak to us, offering their treasures as worthy substitutes for regrets.

And, we should learn from our regrets. As espoused in the television series *Northern Exposure,* we should live each day as if we are about to take off into space. Each morning—and each evening—we should do a pre-flight check, asking ourselves if we are prepared to lift off. Part of that preparation is to not leave undone what we would not want others to bear as regrets. The serendipity of such living is inward peace and serenity.

When I am overwhelmed with regret, I will pause for a moment and remember all of the wonderful times we shared.

Chapter 5

The Little Rituals

The evenings were the hardest to bear. The ritual of the hot drink, the lumps of sugar for the two dogs, the saying of prayers — his boyhood habit carried on throughout our married life — the good night kiss. I continued the ritual, because this too lessened pain, and was, in its poignancy, a consolation.

--Daphne du Maurier

Like du Maurier, I continued rituals I had with my husband. Each evening after getting into bed, we went through a routine:

BOB: *"Night, Sherry. I love you."*

SHERRY: *"Night, Bob. I love you, too."*

BOB: *"Say your prayers."*

SHERRY: *"OK, darling."*

BOB: *"Remember Kevin."*

SHERRY: *"I will. You, too."*

And then, in words whose written form can never convey the cherished inflections, Bob would whisper, almost in awe, "Our favorite time of day," and I would respond with a deep sigh of contentment, "I . . . know."

Next, we said together the Lord's Prayer and the 23rd Psalm before praying our individual prayers silently.

I still go through the ritual—I just say Bob's words as well as mine. Sometimes it makes me cry, but I do it anyway because it was part of our life that we treasured.

Writing about du Maurier's loss of her husband, the author of her obituary said, in an unconscious effort to ease her pain, she had at first taken over some of his things for herself. She wore his shirts, sat at his desk, and used his pen to answer hundreds of letters of condolence. By this process, du Maurier came to feel closer to "Boy Browning," as her husband was called.

Like du Maurier, I wear Bob's favorite fleece jacket, sit in his chair, and sleep on his side of the bed —each an effort to feel closer to him.

We all have rituals and routines, and there is no need to abandon them after our loved one is gone. They can bring comfort, and —at least for a moment— relieve our feeling of aloneness. Yes, others may think we are crazy, but we are not. We are staying in touch with the life we shared. And if wearing our loved one's clothing or continuing lifelong habits helps us feel the presence of our spouse, then why not?

When the physical departure leaves us bereft, we can play a recording in our head of the tender moments we shared, remembering the closeness and love. Picturing the smiling face, the birthdays, and other happy times may at first deepen our grief. In time, though, the scenes will remind us how fortunate we were to have had whatever time we spent with a divine gift that has now been taken back for reasons we cannot understand.

In "The Smoke Jumper," Nicholas Evans wrote that "All of the gathered riches of our journey, the moments shared, the mysteries explored, the steady layering of intimacy stored, the things that made us laugh or weep or sing, the joy of sunlit snow or first unfurling of the spring, the wordless language of look and touch, the knowing, each giving and each taking...are not flowers that fade, nor trees that fall and crumble.... What we were, we are. What we had, we have." I am comforted by Evans' words that, "Just as death is part of life, the dead live on forever in the living." He concludes by asking us to be still and close our eyes — to listen for our loved one's footfall in our heart. "I am not gone but merely walk within you."

For a few moments each day, I will remember something special I shared with my spouse and be thankful. And I will feel my loved one's presence at my side.

Chapter 6

Why Doesn't the World Stop?

And can it be that in a world so full and busy, the loss of one weak creature makes a void in my heart, so wide and deep that nothing but the width and depth of eternity can fill it up!

--Charles Dickens

With a broken heart, we watch as the world continues to spin on its axis. People go shopping, out to eat, to ballgames, to work, and on and on. And yet we sit, immobilized by our grief.

I remember one day when I forced myself to get out of my husband's recliner where I had sat for days, staring into space, and go to a shopping mall. Walking from my car, I felt enveloped in a filmy bubble—I could see out but the people scurrying about seemed distant, as if I were looking at them from another world. In the mall, my feet shuffled through the process of walking, but it was like watching my body and those about me from afar. I felt drugged, not dazed but almost in a fog. My vacant stare invited no approach—I was preoccupied, seeing the people in front of me but not seeing them. Withdrawn into myself, I felt as alone as I have ever felt, even though I was surrounded by hundreds. Half of me was missing, but no one seemed to notice.

Sips of Sustenance

When we go out with family or friends, their easy banter, the natural laughter of close companions, can leave us resentful. How can others so easily forget the loved one who is missing? How can they not see that the world is standing still? We walk beside them, sit beside them, listen to them, but it's like seeing through a glass darkly.

What shall we do? Sit alone forever? Decline all invitations to re-enter the world? Perhaps for a while. As Samuel Johnson said, "While grief is fresh, every attempt to divert only irritates." But the time will come when we should force ourselves to engage in activities with others. Johnson advises us on the timing: "You must wait till it [grief] be digested, and then amusement will dissipate the remains of it." Only we know when our grief is "digested," and only we know when to return to the world of the living.

We will not be instantly happy again. We may never be whole again. But, as George Eliot advised, we can get to the place where we "no longer wrestle with our grief." Where we can "sit down with it as a lasting companion and make it a sharer in our thoughts."

We can look at the world for both our loved one and ourselves. We can see a rainbow and enjoy its beauty for both of us. We can hear a choir of birds for two. We can watch the sun rise in splendor over the ocean for our spouse and ourselves, as we would have stood together, entranced by its beauty. We don't prefer to do it that way, but it's a better choice than not enjoying the wonders of the world ever again.

Yes, the world continues to spin, despite our grief. It won't stop for us to get through our grief, but it will allow us to jump back on when we are ready.

Who would have thought the loss of just one human being could leave such a void? And who would think the chasm will close? But it can, if we can look into our hearts and see we are weeping for what has brought us such great joy. We don't need to suppress our grief, but we do need to temper it with thankful hearts for the time we had together. And while sorrow may be mitigated if we grieved during the extended suffering of our mate, the final parting is still difficult. For many, regardless of the circumstances surrounding death, the intensity of grief is directly related to the intensity of the love that was shared. We should be grateful we had so much to lose. What we had was worth living for, and now it is worth the pain of loss.

In the midst of my deepest grief, I can

pause for a few moments and be thankful

I had such a great gift to lose.

Chapter 7

Platitudes

Everyone can master a grief except he who has it.

--William Shakespeare

Shakespeare was right. Others can tell us how to handle our grief, but until they have walked in our shoes, their words come across as meaningless. Advice abounds, and the worst parts are the pat answers, the platitudes—assurances intended to be genuine but that sometimes sound like inane clichés. "He's in a better place." "She's better off now." "Be glad she's no longer suffering." "She wouldn't want to return to earth." "He wouldn't want you to grieve." "You'll be with him again someday." And on and on... While all of the statements may be true, they can come across as trite and disingenuous when our lives have been torn asunder by loss.

People are trying to be helpful, but sometimes they don't understand the depth of desolation is so great we can't see the wisdom of the words. Knowledge we accepted and trusted is no longer sufficient to address the questions flowing unbidden through our minds. As Ralph Waldo Emerson said, "Sorrow makes us all children again—destroys all differences of intellect. The wisest know nothing." What we once knew for certain, we now question.

Not wanting to hear platitudes doesn't mean disowning our beliefs, but concrete questions about what happens after death may emerge with a fierceness that can't be suppressed. What we once accepted through faith—through a mirror dimly—we now need to be tangible.

When unanswered questions force their way into our consciousness, we should not stifle them. We must face them head on, acknowledging that not only we, but no one, can speak from experience about what happens after death. It's okay to wonder, to ponder, to search for answers, but at some point we should let go. Surely, in a world as intricately and magnificently created as the one in which we live, there is an unseen plan that is just as marvelous for life after death. If an iris is reborn every spring, then we can hope an infinitely more precious human being deserves a similar fate. Momentarily submersed in doubt, our belief in Corinthians, which tells us we now only know in part but will someday know more fully, will eventually resurface.

I will allow myself to ask questions. I will

acknowledge I will never know all of the

answers, but I believe in a master plan in

which my loved one holds a precious part.

Chapter 8

Wearing Masks

There is a quality even meaner than outright ugliness or disorder, and this meaner quality is the dishonest mask of pretended order, achieved by ignoring or suppressing the real order that is struggling to exist and to be served.

--Jane Jacobs

It is a sad truth that in the midst of our deepest grief, we feel the need to don a mask, to further isolate ourselves. Those who have young children sometimes try to hide their feelings, attempting to avoid adding to the trauma their sons or daughters are already experiencing through the loss of a parent. With adolescents, who regularly struggle with mood changes, the surviving parent may sidestep sharing innermost feelings, frightened it will intensify the teen's grief.

Even in the absence of the above situations, we may put up a front when talking with friends and family, hesitant to let them know the depth of our grieving. If asked how we are, we say, "Fine," or "Okay," while inside we are far from either. Yearning to express our sadness, we hold back, not wanting others to know how much we are struggling.

Why is it so difficult to let go, to reveal our innermost thoughts? There are as many answers as there are mourners. Some are simply private individuals who can best work their way through grief alone. Others don't want to burden friends and family with their sorrow. Some feel compelled to prove how strong they are. A number think it would be futile to share how they really feel; no one can understand what they are going through. And yet, as Jacobs said, it is a dishonest mask we wear—and it is a mask that does not protect us and often does more harm. Suppressing our true feelings can be dangerous and may lengthen the grieving process. Our grief demands to be served, and we cannot forever deny its existence.

All people wear masks, but sorrow's disguise is especially prone to disintegrate when we most want to camouflage intimate thoughts. Is unveiling innermost thoughts the worst exposure we could face? Victor Hugo reminds us that "Virtue has a veil; vice a mask," suggesting it is more virtuous to be open and honest about our feelings than to conceal them. Behind our mask are personal truths disclosing who we are and what we believe. Do we want to screen that from others?

Sharing how we feel opens the door for others to accept us in our wholeness. And if they are not ready for that, it is their problem, not ours. As Robert Browning avowed, "Truth never hurts the teller."

Even if I feel more comfortable wearing a mask, I will think about lowering it with special friends and family members, allowing them to see the abyss of my grief for a few moments. Such a gesture of openness may be helpful both to them and to me.

Chapter 9

Getting Through Special Days

*The holiest of all holidays are those kept by ourselves in silence
and apart; the secret anniversaries of the heart, when the full
river of feeling overflows...*

--Henry Wadsworth Longfellow

Birthdays, anniversaries, holidays—times we always spent with our loved one. Days of joyous celebration and excitement now become dreaded like a plague of locusts. How will we ever get through special days alone? Is it possible Longfellow's words could be true—that the most sacred days are those we spend alone in silence? Can the river, full of feeling, overflow without overwhelming us?

Few would disagree that most holidays and other special occasions have become so commercialized their true meaning often fades in the midst of lovingly wrapped packages, personalized singing cards, and pleasurable festivities. Even in the hustle and bustle, being with family and friends is central to the celebrations, so how can we make merry alone and in silence?

Philip Andrew Adams asserted, "To many people, holidays are not voyages of discovery, but a ritual of reassurance." Reassurance that we are loved; reassurance that others care; reassurance that others remember us on special days. But can holidays not be more? Can they be used as a voyage of discovery?

What should we look for on such a voyage? What can we discover if we keep a holiday or special occasion "in silence and apart?"

First, the silence can offer a time of contemplation on the real meaning of the occasion, time to reflect why the event is worth celebrating. An anniversary can remind us, in Simone Signoret's words, that hundreds of tiny threads sew people together. Each of those threads linked our life with our spouse. Some threads may be dark and hold dire memories, but most will be bright and colorful threads, reminding us of good times shared as we stitched our lives together. Those threads can be celebrated alone or with others. The choice is ours. For some, being in the midst of family and friends, talking about the threads of life, will bring comfort. But others may wish to heed Longfellow's words.

Like anniversaries, birthdays can call up the passing years we spent with our beloved. We can choose to dwell on those poignant memories rather than yielding to regret that no more will be shared.

Another way to look at birthdays and other occasions is that they aren't really any different from other days; they are just one more day we will miss the one who is gone. If we think of special days as a

24-hour period that will pass, they become less crushing.

At Thanksgiving, we should try not to succumb to what we have lost. Rather, we should focus on what we have had. How much more tragic it would be not to have shared love at all than to lose it. And so, we can be thankful our paths crossed, for however short or long the time may have been.

And then there is Christmas, the most miraculous of all holidays. Augusta Rundel describes it this way: a "magic blanket that wraps itself about us, that something so intangible that it is like a fragrance. It may weave a spell of nostalgia. Christmas may be a day of feasting, or of prayer, but always it will be a day of remembrance—a day in which we think of everything we have ever loved."

In remembering, we can feel once again the mystery of holding our beloved spouse close. Again, we can choose whether that is a treasured memory or one that brings heartache. As Calvin Coolidge said, "Christmas is not a time nor a season, but a state of mind." Henry Van Dyke would add that we should believe, "Love is the strongest thing in the world—stronger than hate, stronger than evil, stronger than death—and that the blessed life which began in Bethlehem nineteen hundred years ago is the image and brightness of the Eternal Love." Then, Van Dyke says, we can keep Christmas. We can cherish the love we shared — we can feel the real spirit of Christmas and hug the hope it brings.

For a few moments before each special occasion, I will pause and be thankful for the treasured times I shared with my spouse. I know it will not be easy, but I will draw strength from tender memories of the love of kindred that filled those days with joy and contentment. I will let the full river of feelings overflow.

Chapter 10

Shadows

Each substance of grief hath twenty shadows.
--William Shakespeare

All around us are reminders of our loved one. We still see him everywhere. Photographs... Favorite paintings... Books... His favorite chair... The desk where she wrote her letters... The remote he always controlled... The sewing basket that sat beside her chair... Golf clubs... Tennis rackets... The mementos of life...and the shadows of grief.

Photographs. They may be everywhere—if we had them in one room or many rooms before death intruded, we see them and memories hit us, hail bouncing off our hearts, repeatedly striking our souls. If we didn't have photographs on display, we may suddenly want them everywhere. We may create a shrine, with a group or groups of photographs, a way to keep our spouse's face from fading in our mind. Ever close.

We touch her favorite paintings. The ones she selected and treasured. We put our hands on his books, trying to feel his touch on them. We sit in her favorite chair, willing her presence to be made known. Or maybe we just feel closer by sitting there. No more is needed.

And then we see the remote. It was always by his side. Now we can control it, but now we don't want to. Now we can watch a whole program without his switching channels back and forth. That brings a swift smile, swallowed by sorrow in an instant. We would give back the remote if we could.

We walk into our bedroom and see the remnants of life. We pick them up with loving hands, stroke them, and hold them close to our heart—a painful comfort. Jareb Teague's brief words are full of wisdom: "Grief punts around joy." And now the tokens of good times are shrouded by grief.

Are these vestiges of our loved one's life helpful or harmful? Only we can decide. For some, clearing the house of special items frees the mind from constant reminders of the loss. For others, having scraps of life, traces of the physical being, keeps us close to our beloved, soothing our sorrow.

Shadows of the life that was, they cannot be swept away like dust. They linger, trailing us wherever we walk. "Reminiscences," George Bernard Shaw said, "make one feel so deliciously aged and sad."

We evoke poignant memories, remember happy times. And then an unseen hand switches the channel, and we see a blank screen. Reminding us the times are no more. Yet they are recorded in our mind, and we replay them every time we see a photograph, touch a special object, or hear a favorite song.

Should we shut off the recording? Do we put away the photographs, change the furniture, and sweep the shadows from the room? Maybe. Just as our loved one was matchless, so is our grief. Only we can decide when and if to rearrange the relics of the life we held so dear.

Thornton Wilder once said, "We live in what is, but we find 1,000 ways not to face it." At some point we must confront where we live, where we see the constant reminders, and tackle the truth—not of our loss, for it is surely truth. We must cope with the reason we continue to surround ourselves with keepsakes. Would we feel guilty if they were put away? Would we sorrow any more or less without them in view? Do they lift us up or pull us down? It is not what is in front of us that matters; it is how we feel about the objects. Do they lock us in the past or give us the key to continued happiness? No one else can make that judgment for us.

Today I will spend a few moments
thinking about the objects in my life that
create shadows. I will walk through those
shadows, feeling their imprint on my soul.
And when I am ready, I will decide
whether the imprint is sufficient without
the inanimate objects.

Chapter 11

Talking About Your Loved One

There is no grief like the grief that does not speak.
--Henry Wadsworth Longfellow

Talking about a husband or wife should occur spontaneously. Although she is no longer physically beside us, the history of our life with her has not been erased. We should speak of him naturally, as if he has gone away for a long trip. We should call her name easily, with no hint of regret. Speaking of our spouse by name, recalling humorous anecdotes, reminiscing about special times, all keep that person close.

Well-meaning friends and family may cautiously avoid talking about the person who has died, fearing it will prime the well of tears, and it may. But that's okay. Grief rises and falls like an ocean wave, and tender memories stir our emotions, sometimes crashing like a white cap. Releasing those emotions heals, even if just for a moment. The other option—holding the grief inside—can be harmful. Shakespeare warned we should "Give sorrow words," because "the grief that does not speak whispers the o'er fraught heart and bids it break."

Giving sorrow words requires more than just talking about our grief, our loss—how much we miss our loved one. Giving sorrow words demands that we talk of our loved one — the person she was, the times we shared, and dreams we hoped to fulfill. We need to talk about the years we planned to spend together. While we should talk about our incredible loss, we should also talk about the past — the good times and the bad.

We need to remember our loved one in his totality. No one is perfect, and to idolize his life is to diminish it. We all have idiosyncrasies, and most of us have warts — parts of our personality of which we aren't always proud. Perhaps our loved one had a temper or was often impatient. Or maybe she was not always kind and helpful. Did we love her any less? Of course not. We need to remember the balance of our beloved's life. That was the life we shared — not an idyllic, fairyland existence where all was blissful. It's tempting to put the less than perfect parts of our loved one aside, remembering only the parts we cherished. But that will only prolong our grief, for we would be grieving a flawless person who never existed.

Just as we should remember the totality of the person we loved, we should not dwell on the negative parts. What purpose is served by accentuating the less than desirable side? We should acknowledge it but not let it take precedence over the positive attributes.

Shakespeare's good sense is worth considering: "What's gone and what's past help should be past grief."

The goal is to remember the person as he was, to reflect on the individual's uniqueness. To forgive the parts that were less than perfect and to celebrate the parts that made our life with her so special.

When I think of my loved one today, I will

be honest with myself, acknowledging

weaknesses and remembering strengths

with a thankful heart.

Chapter 12

Talking to Your Loved One

Where? Where has it gone, that light, that spark, that love that looked into mine? What has it to do with that cold clay. It's here, here, here in my heart. She's in me, around me. Nothing in that clay.

--Anzia Yedierska

For years, perhaps decades, we talked with our beloved: About mundane things and about special subjects. About the day's events and the dreams of the future. About a spectacular sunrise or a striking sunset. About family, friends, and neighbors; and, about our love for one another.

Physical absence doesn't have to change the conversation all that much, because, as Yedierska wrote, the person is still in our heart. So why not talk to the one in our heart? Others may look at us strangely, so we might not want to talk to our loved one when others are present. But alone we can share sights and experiences in words similar to what we did when our spouse was alive.

Driving down the highway and seeing brilliantly orange poppies, I am compelled to say aloud, "Oh, Bob. Look. Aren't the poppies magnificent?" Watching his dog suffer from cancer, I asked him what he would have me do. Standing on the balcony of our oceanfront condo watching a fishing boat listing in the distance, I point it out to Bob. Daily, I share such moments with him. Does he answer? Of course not, but I talk with him to share—not to receive. Nothing I experience is quite whole if I can't share it with Bob. So I talk to him.

Emily Dickinson told us, "Dying is a wild night and a new road." And it is. But we don't have to leave our shared talks behind—we can take them with us on the new byway. At first, talking to our loved one may make us sadder, but eventually it will come naturally if we keep trying. Like rituals, the one-way conversations will develop a comfortable rhythm and routine.

Today I will try talking to my beloved—I

will share my thoughts, what I feel, and

what I see. I know he is somewhere,

listening.

Chapter 13

Dreams

I think we dream so we don't have to be apart so long. If we're in each other's dreams, we can be together all of the time.

--Thomas Hobbes

Some people dream of their spouse.

Others desperately wish they could.

The truth is we all dream—some of us just can't remember nighttime visions. And, oh, how we would like to if they would bring our loved ones back into our sight, even if only in an ethereal mist in the dark of night. To dream that our husband or wife is still alive brings a temporary reprieve—a time when we can be joyful rather than filled with sorrow. Overwhelmed by our loss, we will take any escape we can, however brief it may be, if the dreams put the person back in a state of wellness and life.

Occasionally, though, the dreams are not so pleasant. They depict our loved one in danger, or they might fill us with a sense of being overcome, perhaps similar to being smothered by a pillow pushed against our face or the face of our beloved. Some dream of being adrift on the ocean, unable to return to shore. Another might dream of being lost in a wilderness with no hope of finding a way out. Still another may have a sense of drowning. Such dreams leave us shaken, distressed by our inability to help our loved one or ourselves.

Sips of Sustenance

It may help our dreams be sweet ones if we imagine our husband or wife in safety and security before we lie down to sleep. We can go through photographs and mementos, capturing happy times together, imprinting the loving times in our consciousness. We can't compel a dream or demand what its contents may be, but it doesn't hurt to try to give dreams a framework in which to form.

However dreams develop, many people see them as signs their loved ones are not gone forever. Someone once said dreams are bad because all they do is leave the truth behind. I believe they help us remain connected with our spouse. Maybe we can use them to say the goodbye we missed being able to express. In their book on grief, Kubler-Ross and Kessler tell us, "Dreams can become a meeting place between the world of the living and the realm of the deceased."

Even more far reaching, as Victor Hugo declared, a dream can be used to create the future. If we dream of our loved one restored to good health or in a state of contentment, we can use that illusion to help us get through our grief—to enable us to allow ourselves to let go and live again. The dream can free us to face the future.

Virginia Woolf avowed, "...it is in our idleness, in our dreams, that the submerged truth sometimes comes to the top." If we hang on to repressed beliefs in life after death through dreams, what better result?

Dreams

In my sorrow, if I dream of my loved one, I will be grateful when I awaken that I have seen him again.

Chapter 14

Signs or Messages from Your Loved One

In the night, hope sees a star, and listening love can hear the rustle of a wing.

--Russell Ingersoll

We have all heard stories of footsteps on the staircase, unusually bright stars in the dark night sky, and other unexplained phenomena. Some time ago one of my sisters told me about a friend whose husband's name appeared on her cell phone caller ID months after he had died. He had never had a cell phone and the caller ID on their land line had been changed to her name, so where his name came from on her phone was a mystery, And yet, there it was, the letters clearly etched on her own cell phone screen. How can such an incident be explained? Was it her husband reaching out to her from death to tell her he was okay? Obviously, in a similar circumstance, most people would harbor such a hope.

In my own case, I had two experiences that made me wonder if my husband were trying to reassure me. For many years, we were enthralled with trains, loving to ride the rails in Europe. In America, we took pleasure in hearing the whistle of a distant freight train. It became a game for us anytime we heard or saw a train—one of us would start and the other would pipe in, in a voice of joy and wonderment: "Oh, boy, oh boy, oh boy, oh boy. A train, a train, a train, a train."

After we moved following my retirement, I don't recall ever hearing a train whistle from our new home until the night my husband died. As I lay awake in the wee hours of the morning with my heart shattered, after having discovered his deathly cold body that afternoon, I heard the faint sound of a train in the distance. Stunned, I sat up in bed and listened carefully, but I didn't hear it again. Over the next few months, I heard trains in the middle of the night once or twice a week. And then they stopped. Were they a sign from my beloved that all was well with him, and when he thought I no longer needed to hear the trains, they no longer ran? I don't know, but at the time the sounds of trains in the distance comforted my heart. Many times my husband had told me if he died first, he would try to let me know he was all right. I like to think he was the conductor on those trains.

I am not a person who believes in the paranormal. I am practical, down-to-earth, and sensible. But the trains—and an exceptionally brilliant star—pierced my stalwart pragmatism and made me wonder.

Signs or Messages from Your Loved One

An independent and successful career woman, I was brought to my knees by my husband's death. Night after night, day after day, I struggled with accepting the finality of losing him. And, I wanted to know that he was safe. That he had made it across the great divide and was in a new home far surpassing anything on earth. So maybe I was vulnerable to signs, as many people are.

As I took my daily walk each evening, I asked my husband to keep his promise — to show me he was okay. And then, one night I looked up and saw the brightest star I had ever seen. For a while, it was the only star in the sky. As I walked, it moved with me, following me from one end of my walk to the other. Astounded, I would stop to see if the star stopped, and it did. When I began to walk again, it started moving again. If I turned in a different direction, it also turned. Mystified and astounded, I called my sister to come and see if she saw what I saw. And she did — the movement of the star with each step we took rendered us speechless. (It was so eerie it actually frightened her.) This continued for months wherever I went. Even traveling back from a trip in another region of the state, I saw the star as I crossed over a mountain, and it stayed in front of me until I was safely home. When I went to our Florida condo, I could see the star as I stood on the balcony during the late evening. Wherever I went, the intense, dazzling star was there—the first one in the sky each night. And then, like the train, it was gone.

We are all faced with the mystery of what happens after death. Regardless of the strength of our spiritual beliefs, the question is unanswerable. Those who say they know the answer delude themselves, for they haven't experienced the unknown. There are theories, many of them based on Biblical verses and stories, but they are sometimes confusing and contradictory.

Many people thus resort to psychic mediums, hoping they can provide the answer to what happened to their loved ones. One such woman was at first skeptical as she listened to a weekly show "Crossing Over" by John Edward, but eventually she became fascinated. Describing her own belief system as "weak but hopeful," she tells about signs the medium receives from his mother, usually white feathers found in unusual places. Deciding to try her own experiment, over a period of three weeks she asked her deceased father, grandmother, and others to send a black feather. Highly specific, she wanted it left in her front yard. One Sunday, she found a black feather on its edge, tucked into a small space between grass and the edge of the sidewalk. Just a black feather, she says, but it caused her heart to stop. Dumbfounded, she still doesn't know if the feather was a "message" from heaven, but like the signs I treasured, it brought comfort.

Unexplainable events related to the death of loved ones are sprinkled throughout the Internet and abound in books about life after death—stories that touch the heart despite apparent coincidences we interpret as signs. One such book cites 353 ADCs (after death communications) of the more than 3,300 first-hand accounts the authors claim to have collected from people who believe a deceased loved one has contacted them.

Sometimes ADCs come spontaneously as a gift; other times they come in response to a prayer. Traditionally, butterflies are one of the most common signs, followed by rainbows, flowers, and birds. Whether the sign comes almost immediately after death or months later, most people seem to intuitively realize it is a sign sent for a specific purpose just for them.

History is replete with famous people who encountered the dead in life. In the 1700s, John Wesley, founder of the Methodist Church, reportedly had lively conversations with the dead in his dreams. Centuries later, Peter Sellers is said to have talked often with his dead mother. Author Norman Vincent Peale, noted for his positive-thinking messages, avowed he had glimpses of cherished family members on several occasions.

Sophocles once said, "Grief teaches the steadiest minds to waver," and perhaps that is what is happening when otherwise "normal" people succumb to the temptation of believing in the paranormal. Or perhaps the wavering is the door to another level of consciousness.

Each day, I will be open to signs my loved one is safe and content. I will be thankful for "messages" others may see as coincidences or nothing out of the ordinary, for they will comfort my grieving heart. And if they aren't messages, if they help me, does it really matter?

Chapter 15

Weeping Birds and Elephants

*Did you ever see a robin weep when leaves begin to die? That
means he's lost the will to live. I'm so lonesome I could cry.*
--Hank Williams

The old Hank Williams song describes a robin, but
it was a white-winged, weeping dove my husband
and I once watched for over an hour as it hung its
head, walking round and round its dead mate. In the
city square of Brussels, surrounded by buildings
several hundred years old, we were held captive by
the distressed dove who kept vigil over his loved
one's broken body. Finally, we let the dove outlast us,
and we moved on our way. I've always wondered
how long the lovely yet pitiful bird stood there
mourning, perhaps hoping—if he just waited long
enough—his mate would rise up, her wings once
again carrying her away with him.

Those of us who have lost a loved one can identify
with the dove and the robin. Like Williams, we have
heard the lonesome whippoorwill, too blue to fly, sing
desolately in our hearts, and we have listened to the
mournful sounds of the midnight train "whining
low."

In the midst of such somber sounds as we grieve,
it is tempting to follow the lead of the robin in

Williams' song, losing the will to live. In the long night hours, "when time goes crawling by," we want to hide behind the clouds, like the moon, to cry and bewail our loss.

Mourning is a part of life. Birds, humans, even elephants, express grief. One of my favorite books is *Why Elephants Weep*, because it describes so vividly that emotions are not limited to humans. With illustrations from elephants to dogs to chimpanzees and more, authors Masson and McCarthy describe the depth and breadth of emotions displayed by non-humans. Anecdotes of sorrowful creatures flow heartbreakingly across the pages of the book.

If lamenting the loss of one we love is pathos we share with all created beings, is our only choice to succumb to the deafening roar of loneliness? Choosing to surrender to the pathos and losing our will to live?

Being alone does not always result in loneliness. "Alone" is defined as being without any other person physically nearby. In contrast, "lonely" is described as feeling sad whether by oneself or with companions. Having no one beside us doesn't necessitate sadness forever. Being alone does not demand feeling empty and lost. Rather, we can "transform the emptiness of loneliness to the fullness of aloneness," as Sunita Khosia said, who adds in wonderment, "Ah, that is the secret of life." Khosia believes we can be without sadness — and even be content and at peace with ourselves — if we can only find a way to be comfortable with being alone.

At first, I didn't know how to exist in a world where my beloved didn't. Then one day, in an epiphany, I realized I *was* existing. It was that I didn't know how to *live* in a world where Bob didn't.

Finding the will to live — not just exist — is the beginning of the journey from loneliness to aloneness. Like elephants, robins, doves, and countless other creatures, we will find *life* on the other side of the tunnel of grief. Time will, as Williams crooned, go "crawling by," but it does go by. And in time, we may find we no longer want to hide behind the clouds, like the moon. We will see, as Williams' song promises, that the silence of a falling star will light up the purple sky.

I will pause for a few moments today and
refuse to allow loneliness to overwhelm
me. In its place, I will make space for
aloneness, letting it fill me with solace.

Chapter 16

Loneliness

We're born alone, we live alone, we die alone. Only through love and friendship can we create the illusion for the moment that we're not alone.

--Orson Welles

We cherish the illusion Welles describes, even if it is only for the moment. And when the illusion is gone, we ache in its absence. It's not just the physical loneliness; it's much more than that. It's the missing soul connection—the indefinable affinity we feel with another human being. The bond between husband and wife, connecting both body and soul, cannot be replicated. Severed by death, the connection is irreparably broken with the last breath of life.

Sometimes I think I sit in my husband's recliner not just to try to feel his presence but also to avoid looking at the empty chair. To prevent the image of his sitting there, marker in hand as he underlined a passage in the book he was reading. To circumvent remembering how he used to look over at me, sometimes with steely blue eyes, and read me the words he had marked.

Now I'm alone. Without the person I loved with all my heart.

Sips of Sustenance

I can identify with Samuel Johnson's sense of abandonment: "I have ever since [his wife's death] seemed to myself broken off from mankind; a kind of solitary wanderer in the wild of life, without any direction, or fixed point of view; a gloomy gazer on the world to which I have little relation."

Aimless. Lost. No road to follow. No map to guide; no hand to push us into action.

In a mundane sense, the loss of a spouse leaves us on our own to move furniture, take the dog out, light the fire, change the light bulb, sew on a button, water the flowers, cook our own meals. Without help, make all the decisions, both big and small. Yes, these are all things that can be learned; it's the feeling of being alone that's inescapable, that can't be defined in words others comprehend, that hangs heavy in the silence of absence. We know what Mother Teresa meant when she avowed, "The most terrible poverty is loneliness."

Sometimes we cherish loneliness. When friends drain us with words and hovering, we may look forward to times alone, when we can sit openly with grief as our sole companion. In gentler times, we found beauty in solitude, in watching a burnished orange sunset alone, in feeling the brush of wind on our shoulders, in touching a velvety rose. But then it was a choice. Now aloneness comes unbidden, shrouding us as it threatens to smother what's left of our life.

Paul Tillich, a German-born theologian and philosopher, once said, "Language...has created the word 'loneliness' to express the pain of being alone. And it has created the word 'solitude' to express the glory of being alone." How can we move from loneliness to solitude? Is it possible? Perhaps, but we must each find our own way. Some find their spirits refreshed sitting by the side of a quiet lake. Others seek solace on a mountaintop, where they feel close to the heavens. Maya Angelou found refuge in music: "I could crawl into the spaces between the notes and curl my back to loneliness." For each of us, a way exists to move from loneliness to solitude. We just have to find it.

Dag Hammarskjold challenged us to "pray that our loneliness may spur us into finding something to live for, great enough to die for." If we accept the challenge, in finding something worth living for we may also find we are no longer bound by loneliness when we are alone. A sense of worth, a feeling of value outside us can bring solace even when our loved one is no longer at our side.

Loneliness makes us feel forsaken, but it is a part of every man, woman, and child. Thomas Wolfe described it this way: "The whole conviction of my life now rests upon the belief that loneliness, far from being a rare and curious phenomenon, peculiar to myself and to a few other solitary men, is the central and inevitable fact of human existence."

We are not alone in our loneliness if it is central to every person's existence. Whether it remains loneliness or is transformed into solitude is a choice each individual must make.

In the quiet of this evening, I will seek

solitude, allowing peace to replace pain for

a few moments.

Chapter 17

Losses

I wanted a perfect ending. Now I've learned, the hard way, that some poems don't rhyme, and some stories don't have a clear beginning, middle, and end. Life is about not knowing, having to change, taking the moment and making the best of it, without knowing what's going to happen next.

--Gilda Radner

The loss of our spouse is not the only loss we must bear. Sometimes a new grief dredges up old ones. We remember losses we have endured in years past. In some cases, we may have shortchanged the grieving process, and old griefs resurrect themselves in our present state of sorrow. As painful as this is, it may help us to excise the hurt, to work our way through the throes of the old death. This time, perhaps, we can find our way to wholeness.

If we don't have unresolved losses to deal with, the death of our loved one still brings an abundance of losses. Sometimes we no longer feel comfortable with the friends we shared with our husband or wife. If most of our friends were married couples, being with these friends, watching them exchange loving looks, holding hands, or even kissing strikes like a javelin in our hearts. Even in the absence of such intimacies, just seeing people in two's when we are one may be a constant reminder of our loss.

If our financial circumstances change with the death of our spouse, we may also lose the home we shared. We may move across town or across the country to be closer to family. We may move from a large home to a small apartment. If we must move at all, regardless of where we go and what kind of home we will have, we are thrown into an unknown environment. Such change in the midst of bereavement adds to our distress.

Those fortunate enough to stay in our homes still face losses. Loss of the person we had meals with around the kitchen table; the person with whom we went to movies, to church, to restaurants, to ballgames; the person with whom we bowled, swam, played bridge or golf; the person with whom we sat companionably, watching television and eating popcorn. All of the small and large activities we took for granted made up a large part of our lives, and now they are gone.

Another loss to absorb is our dream for the future. Plans, concrete or fantasy, have been swallowed like minnows scooped up by a diving seagull. The future we face has been irrevocably changed. The face of our spouse forever erased from the days and years ahead. Voyages we had planned never to be realized.

Gardens to be tilled left idle. Birthdays or anniversaries to be celebrated in days of sorrow. We know what Norman Cousins meant when he said, "Death is not the greatest loss in life. The greatest loss is what dies within us while we live."

The choice is ours. We can sit, as Walter Anderson said, "in perpetual sadness, immobilized by the gravity of [our] loss, or [we] can choose to rise from the pain and treasure the most precious gift [we] have —life."

Looking at our future is like gazing at a silhouette. No substance, just a dark shadow.

How do we add light and color to the silhouette? How do we envision a life more than half full? Perhaps it would be helpful to think of building a bridge from our past life with our loved one to a new life without our spouse. For a while, we may not be able to visualize that future, but we can start laying the foundation. Later, we can add planks on the bridge, and piece-by-piece, we will move toward a new life. What that life will be like may be unknown right now, but if we build the bridge, it will lead us someplace we may never have envisioned. Not the same as the life we had planned with our loved one. Different yes; nevertheless, a life worth living.

As I deal with my loss, I will take a
moment or two each day to contemplate
how I can build a bridge to my future.

Chapter 18

The Strong Made Weak

Tell me, how can I live without my husband any longer? This is my first awakening thought each morning, and as I watch the waves of the turbulent lake under our windows, I sometimes feel I should like to go under them.

--Mary Todd Lincoln

Death strikes with a blow that could fell the largest redwood tree in the forest. One that can stagger even the hardiest of souls. We've all known people who never recover from the death of a spouse, and it's easy to assume they were just weak people. But we expect those who have demonstrated inner strength on past occasions to bear the new burden with faith and positive thinking. After all, Winston Churchill avowed, "We shall draw from the heart of suffering itself the means of inspiration and survival." But death's finality brings a new dimension to anguish because—at least in this life—there is no hope for reversing our loss, no anticipation our loved one will return. Where within that suffering, Mr. Churchill, can we discover inspiration and the will to survive?

Drowning in tears, hearts torn open, and the strength we once wore like armor now rusted and buried in desolation, like Mary Lincoln, we question how we can live without our beloved. So at first, we give in to grieving without thought of getting better. But when weeks and months pass and we still feel smothered by our sorrow, we begin to look at ourselves askance. Why can't I accept my loss? Why can't I get a grip and get on with life? Others begin to push us, suggesting we need help, counseling or medication. You can't grieve forever, they say. Offended by the suggestion that we can't handle our emotions, we resolve anew to get control, to become more active, to return to the world of the living.

With time, we think, we will get better. And then more months pass, and we still have such an incredible void in our lives that getting better seems impossible. Oh, we may hide our mourning more effectively, but inside we still ache with each passing day. Time. Why doesn't it bring relief? Because, as Domenico Cieri Estrada said, "Time is like the wind, it lifts the light and leaves the heavy." Grief weighs us down, an anchor of agony filling our lungs until we think they might burst.

How much time before we can face a day without mourning? No one knows, not even we ourselves. We just have to keep plodding along, hoping Faith Baldwin's words were true: "Time is a dressmaker specializing in alterations."

The Strong Made Weak

Our lives have been altered by death, and eventually time will alter our thoughts. But we can't rush the process. We don't have to stop grieving just because it has been a month or three months or even a year or more. We don't have to let others tell us when our sorrow should diminish. Henry David Thoreau spoke with wisdom beyond this earth when he noted we cannot kill time without injuring eternity.

At first, it does seem we may grieve our way into eternity, but we must give grief the space and time it needs to work its way through our heart and soul. And then, one day we will wake up to once again find pleasure in the rising sun, the sound of chirping birds, and the brush of wind—or is it angel's wings—upon our parched face. When will it happen? No one knows, but it will happen if we choose to recognize, in the words of Benjamin Disraeli, that "Grief is the agony of an instant, the indulgence of grief the blunder of life."

It is tempting to indulge our grief forever, but that would be a mistake. We must work our way through grief to the other side, never losing sight of our husband or wife but not letting the loss consume our very being. It is a difficult journey, even for the strong, but unless we want to dwell in the land of sorrow the rest of our lives, it is a passage we must find. How? By learning to smile again at happy memories, to laugh at old jokes we shared, and to hope for a joyous reunion in another life. This transformation won't happen overnight, but when we least expect it, we will glimpse a life where grief doesn't override all other emotions. Where the void in our heart allows new joy to fill tiny crevices. Perhaps never whole again, but not totally broken either.

Although mourning can go on for years and years, Elizabeth Kubler-Ross tells us we must come to grips with death before we can live again. It's a false fantasy, she says, to assume grieving stops after a year. Rather, Kubler-Ross declares it ends when we realize we can live again — when we can concentrate our energies on our lives as a whole, and not on our pain and regrets.

I will allow my grief to run its course, but when kinder emotions surface, I will not suppress them. I will give them room in my heart for a moment or two until I can push more grief aside to make space for the joys of life to return.

Chapter 19

Light and Darkness

You're searching...
For things that don't exist; I mean beginnings.
Ends and beginnings – there are no such things.
There are only middles.

--Robert Frost

Sometimes, lost in our grief, we search for things that don't exist. We look for an easy way to end our sorrow and a quick route to joy again. We search for answers we couldn't understand if we had them. We seek lightness, but its stark brilliance overwhelms us, and we cower back into darkness. We feel safest when we are withdrawn from the world, when we enter caverns of silence and sorrow. Protected by their thick walls, we do not have to think about tomorrow or even how to exist today.

We dwell on our loss, preferring despair to the unknown. Better to be hopeless than to know the worst of what life will be like without our loved one. Nonetheless, we must be careful lest we find, as Anais Nin said, "The time comes when the risk to remain tight in a bud is more powerful than the risk to blossom." We do not wish to become the cold custodian of a purposeless life.

Lost in darkness, it is tempting to refuse to search for a new middle—a different life between the beginning and end of our life—that we never imagined would be needed. But here we sit, with the life we had up to this time vanished in an instant and the life we still have to live stretching before us interminably. Leonard Cohen's words flow through our crushed spirits: "The blizzard of the world...has overturned the order of the soul." What we once held so tightly is gone, lost in the most malevolent storm we have ever encountered. What shall we do with the days and hours we must face without our mate by our side?

We can remain broken, or we can re-splice the shattered parts to find a way to live in the present. We can realize that "Life is a stranger's sojourn, a night at an inn," as Marcus Aurelius penned. Our time here on earth is so short—do we want to waste what is left of it?

What shall the design of a new middle part of our lives look like? The possibilities are limitless if we find the strength to embrace the light, filling it with purposeful activities rather than being blinded by it.

If we can work our way through grief, we will become stronger in the places where we were broken. In that strength—in a new middle—we can once again seek and find peace. We can, as Albert Camus did, "in the depth of winter, finally learn that within [us] there lay an invincible summer."

As I quietly grieve, I will look inside

myself for an indomitable strength to help

me face the sunlight again with hope in

my heart that I will find life again on the

other side of despair.

Chapter 20

Finding Strength in Backwater

Confront the dark parts of yourself, and work to banish them with illumination and forgiveness. Your willingness to wrestle with your demons will cause your angels to sing. Use the pain as fuel, as a reminder of your strength.

--August Wilson

Over the years, we all hit turbulent waters. At times, we become driftwood, floating aimlessly among the backwaters. Sometimes we get caught in debris, tangled and unable to break loose. Losing a husband or wife is like that. We get stuck in our grief, and we wonder if we will ever be free of our sorrow.

When we were in backwater before grief invaded our lives, we could usually summon up happier times. Periods of contentment, which, even with their ups and downs, made us feel we were where we should be. In joy and despair, we believed we were on the right track because our loved one was with us. Even when we were occasionally lost in the river of time, we knew the winds would eventually blow us back on course.

But loss of the person dearest to our heart throws us in backwater so rough we are tempted to let the current pull us under. Even if we resist the tug, we may be content to float unfettered, defying any suggestion that we should get back into the master plan for our lives. Urging from others sinks like quicksand. Only we can decide when we have been in the dark waters long enough for our soul to be replenished.

Elbert Hubbard tells us, "It does not take much strength to do things, but it requires great strength to decide what to do." We need stamina to find the will to continue and endure, to decide how we should live without our beloved.

Can we really use our pain as fuel, as Wilson suggests? Perhaps so, if we accept that our strength does not come from within—if we can believe an unseen force will send the spark of life back into our soul. Only then, as Ralph Waldo Emerson believed, can we find that strength grows out of our weakness. In more common vernacular, we must do what Franklin Roosevelt commanded: "When you get to the end of your rope, tie a knot and hang on."

Tying the knot may not be simple, but when we are at the end of the rope, no other option exists. We must nurture an indomitable will in our quest for strength. With that will, we can confront the dark part of our lives—the loss of our loved one—banishing the sorrow from our consciousness by replacing it with memories that lift us up. Not an easy task, but one we must undertake.

Finding Strength in Backwater

Corrie ten Boom, the Holocaust survivor who helped so many Jews escape, said, "If God sends us on strong paths, we are provided strong shoes." From those strong paths, we will learn strength; and if we survive, we will be stronger for having traversed the route from death back to life.

Most of us are stronger than we think. Though we may temporarily lose control of that strength, we can choose to pull it back up from the depths of our being. When we do that, angels will sing in our hearts again.

In the midst of my grieving, I will find the

strength, even if it is only for a few

moments of time, to listen for melodious

angels again.

Chapter 21

The Laziness of Grief

And no one told me about the laziness of grief...I loathe the slightest effort.

--C.S. Lewis

Grief sucks the wind out of us. We face a journey over unknown terrain, but we are devoid of energy. We have no will to get up and move. Once intensely active, we become sluggards, wanting to do nothing more than sit with a vacant stare on our faces.

If someone would provide a roadmap, we might summon up enough energy to begin our travels. But the passage requires a new map for each sorrowful sojourner, and we have neither the will nor the insight to draw the lines for roads we can follow, mountains we must climb, valleys we will pass through. Lethargic, it is easier to do nothing than something. Others urge us, chastise us, compel us, but we want no part of living.

For a while, idleness may be what we need, but we should be cautious that, as Martin Luther warned, our "not now" does not become "never." Idleness is emptiness and can make us stagnant, unable to bear the fruits of life.

Eleanor Roosevelt rebuked idleness with these words: "So much attention is paid to the aggressive sins, such as violence and cruelty and greed, with all their tragic effects, that too little attention is paid to the passive sins, such as apathy and laziness, which in the long run can have a more devastating effect."

Laziness and idleness differ from resting, which we need to do. Can we not all recall how good it feels to lie down after a hard day of physical labor? Tired and exhausted, rest swathes us like a cool feather bed. This sweet relief comes only after intense activity. As Albert Einstein decried, "The idle man does not know what it is to enjoy rest."

So should we force ourselves from our bed, from our chair? Should we demand of ourselves that we move on? Perhaps, but only when we have been still long enough to let our energy rebuild following the blow we have borne. We should never forget Virginia Wolfe's wisdom: "Yet it is in our idleness, in our dreams, that the submerged truth sometimes comes to the top." As we rest, truth rises to the level of consciousness.

We need to find truth beneath our grief, and if we become too busy too fast, we may miss the enlightenment that may surface as we sit idle.

In the midst of my idleness, I will allow

truth to find its way into my vacant mind.

Chapter 22

Action

The only cure for grief is action.

--George Henry Lewis

Sitting still staring into space is tempting, and it requires so little. But days of nothingness stretch on interminably and if allowed to continue too long, they stymie the grief process. Sorrow must have its time and space, but being totally idle for an excessive amount of time will throw the grieving process into a continuous loop. A broken record, we play and replay the same lines in our waking hours until they echo in our sleep.

If we have a job, returning to work as quickly as possible helps occupy our days, diverting our attention from our loss to the world of living. Work may well be the best medicine for grief. Going back to work isn't easy, and the first few days will be stressful as people with good intentions attempt to express their concern. That will soon pass, and everyone will start treating us normally. Soon, we will slip back into a comfort zone at work where we allow ourselves to temporarily escape from grief while we deal with the more mundane problems of life.

If we don't have a position to which we must report every day, we can still find ways to occupy our time. That may mean going to hospitals to visit people who are suffering. It may require volunteering with a hospice group. Or, it may just demand we clean our home or garage with a fury. Other activities that may help include reading—perhaps about the grieving process or about life after death, or on a totally different subject that forces us to concentrate for a few moments on world affairs, a good novel, or travel. Some find that keeping a journal of their thoughts helps. Putting words on paper propels us through our turmoil of thoughts and has the potential to serve as a catharsis.

Grief, Samuel Johnson avers, is a "species of idleness." When idle, our thoughts drift toward our bereavement, our regrets, and our future alone. When occupied productively, we move beyond ourselves into a world that hasn't stopped with our loss. Alone, sitting silently, life hangs heavy upon us. As Joseph Addison wrote in *Cato*, describing how Marcus felt about the absence of Lucia: "I am ten times undone, while hope, and fear, and grief, and rage, and love rise up at once. And with variety of pain distract me."

We can choose to be distracted by our grief, our rage, our lost love, and our pain, or we can choose to be distracted by something in the world of the living. It's hard to think about our sorrow when engaged in activities that demand our attention. Yes, the angst will return when we are alone, but at least we had a respite.

The grieving process is hell, so we should heed the words of Churchill: "If you're going through hell, keep going."

Action

I will not allow myself to sit idle too long.

Each day, I will force myself to engage in

some activity requiring my mind to think

of something besides my loss. As I can, I

will increase the time I spend in such

activities.

Chapter 23

Returning to Life

Loss is nothing else but change, and change is Nature's delight.
--Marcus Aurelius,
Meditations

When we can sit no longer, walking may help. Physical exercise is therapeutic, and if weather permits, being surrounded by nature's artistry can make us mindful of the cyclical movement of life and death. A newly sprouted crocus or tulip speaks of rebirth, and trees dressed in bright green leaves of spring are visible proof that from death comes life.

It's tempting to think spring is the best season, but we may even find solace in summer's searing heat, allowing it to melt our grief for a time. As the heat retreats, gentle fall breezes are transformed into angel wings, fanning our parched souls. Despite our sorrow, we may find winter has its own beauty in the snowflakes dancing gracefully outside our window. We may discover, as Andrew Wyethe did, that we prefer fall and winter, "...when you feel the bone structure in the landscape—the loneliness of it—the dead feeling of winter. Something waits beneath it—the whole story doesn't show." So it is that something lies below the winter of grief—the rest of the story of our life waiting to unfold—to spring forth from our frozen being.

William Browne, writing in *Variety* in 1630, noted that "There is no season such delight can bring, as summer, autumn, winter and the spring." Every season brings its own message of death and rebirth—the whole story. If nature is reborn every year in predictable cycles, is it not possible our loved one has been transformed into new life?

The natural world speaks of a master design—the tides move in concert with the moon, and the sun is the exact distance from earth to give light but not set it afire. A man and woman's bodies were designed to fit together in an amazing way to produce new life. And there are countless other remarkable dimensions and angles in the blueprint. In the presence of such a magnificent and intricately interwoven creation, is it not likely our spouse continues to have a place?

For a moment, this reassurance may lessen our grief, but it is only a temporary reprieve. The absence of our mate cuts us, a tree savaged by a storm. Crashing to the ground, the limbs entangle us, and we are once again caught in the throes of grief.

Will it never end? In the first few days and months, it seems not. Some people try to tell us that once we go through a year and all of the special occasions it brings, we will be better. But there is no set timetable for grief. For some, not even a year or more brings relief. The future stretches in front of us interminably, and facing the days ahead without our spouse seems unbearable.

We no longer feel whole—a piece of us has been ripped out and the gaping hole the loss created may scab over for a short time, but again and again we pick at the thin layer covering the wound until the bleeding returns. As Washington Irving said, "The sorrow for the dead is the only sorrow from which we refuse to be divorced. Every other wound we seek to heal, every other affliction to forget, but this wound we consider it a duty to keep it open; this affliction we cherish and brood over in solitude."

At some point, we recognize we may never get over the loss of our husband or wife. But what we can do is get through the grief, one moment at a time. We can take the little escapes—a memory that brings a smile to our face, a friend who drops by with a freshly baked cake, a walk in a rain shower that washes the tears from our face—and hold them close. They won't last long, but they give us breathing space, a little air in our lungs before the next wave of grief smothers us. With time, the waves get further apart, separated by longer respites of diversions distracting us from our grief. We do not have to feel guilty—our loved one would not want us to dwell in the land of sorrow forever.

Percy Bysshe Shelley wrote, "Winter is come and gone, but grief returns with the revolving year." And it does. Thankfully, though, while time may not heal, as the months pass, the pain is softer, more tolerable. Daphne du Maurier described it this way: "As the seasons change, something of tranquility descends, and although the well-remembered footstep will not sound again, nor the voice call from the room beyond, there seems to be about one in the air an atmosphere of love, a living presence. . .it is as though one shares, in some indefinable manner, the freedom and peace, even at times the joy, of another world where there is no more pain. The feeling is simply there, pervading all thought, all action. When Christ the healer said, 'Blessed are they that mourn, for they shall be comforted,' he must have meant just this."

Just for a moment, today I will walk

outside and look for nature's message that

life goes on.

Chapter 24

Unexpected Surges of Grief

Like love, grief fades in and out.

--Mason Cooley

Just when we think we have conquered our emotions, that we can control our tears, in an instant grief overwhelms us, and we lose it. It's strange, we can resist succumbing to tears for days, sometimes even in the first hours of grief when we don't want to fall apart in front of friends and family. Even if we let our sorrow flow during that time, we eventually get to a stage where we can hold back the raging tide. And then, an unexpected greeting, a kind word, a special song, the sighting of a flower our loved one cherished, and we are back in the depths of despair, emotions unleashed — a torrent spilling over a dam.

A number of months after my husband died, I forced myself to go to the home of one of my sisters for a family gathering. By reigning in my feelings, I had been able to smile a bit and talk with family members throughout the afternoon. It wasn't easy, but I managed. Then, when I told everyone I had to leave to check on my husband's sheepdogs and my brother-in-law offered to do it for me so I could visit longer, I lost it. I barely made it to my car before the tears flowed, and I choked back racking sobs all the way home. Later, when I told my sister kindnesses were hard to bear, that knowing my usually unconcerned brother-in-law had pity for me touched and saddened me. She told her husband and the next time I called, he was intentionally gruff. We had a good laugh about that, but the fact remained that thoughtful, caring words often touch a tender chord and grief not only fades in, it picks up steam and runs roughshod over our well-steeled demeanor. Bede Jarrett said it well: "Sorrow we can hold, however desolating, if nobody speaks to us. If they speak, we break down."

Inevitably, we all run into people we have not heard from since the death of our beloved. And, of course, they feel compelled to express their sympathy. It's hard not to yell—if you didn't care enough to contact me when she died, why bother to say anything now? Even if we refrain from such an intemperate response, sympathetic words often dredge up the overwhelming sense of loss we had somehow managed to suppress for a time.

Why is it that compassion hurts more than cruelty? I'm not sure, but I know it is true. And I know that grief ebbs and flows, just not with the set rhythm of the ocean tides. Rather, it hits as a tsunami, unexpectedly and with a force so ferocious it throws us backward into the hell of grief just when we see a peek of shoreline over the rim of the horizon. We don't need to be disturbed by the pace, three steps forward and two steps backward. Even with the setbacks, we can make progress in getting through grief.

I will not be dismayed by surges of sorrow. I will accept the ebb and flow of grief as part of the process of getting through my loss and be grateful for the moments when grief ebbs before it flows again.

Chapter 25

When You Least Expect It

My heart leaps when I see a rainbow in the sky.

--William Wordsworth

Just when we think we are climbing out of the depths of grief, we are thrown into free fall again, hitting the bottom with a resounding thump. Sometimes we know what throws us in rebound; other times the sorrow sinks us without reason.

Occasionally, though, the opposite happens. When we are at our lowest, something appears to lift us up. Early one evening while I was sitting, mindlessly watching television, I looked up and saw the most glorious rainbow I had ever witnessed. Drawn outside, I walked onto the balcony and stepped to the edge. In front of me, one end of the rainbow rose from the dark blue ocean, rays of azure, rose, gold, and emerald so splendid they took my breath away. My eyes followed the vivid, multihued arch high into the heavens and back down into the ocean miles away. I stood transfixed for what seemed hours, my eyes traversing from one end of the rainbow to the other, time and time again.

Goethe was wrong when he said that after fifteen minutes no one looks at a rainbow any more. I'm not sure what compelled me, but I could not go inside as long as the rainbow glowed hoveringly in the sky. And then it began to grow fainter on one end, and I watched it ever so slowly fade into the sky. When I looked toward the other end, the glowing paint strokes still brushed the sea. Again, I stood mesmerized by the rainbow's translucent beauty, even though it was half of the whole.

And then I thought about my feeling that I was half of what I used to be. Like the rainbow, one part had disappeared into a mist and left the other half hanging, reaching into the heavens but still stroking the earth. As the second half of the rainbow began to pale and lose color where it touched the ocean, I watched the vibrant hues grow fainter and fainter as they stretched their arms toward the sky, until they, too, disappeared into the heavens.

Still searching for peace, longing for assurance I would be joined again with the one I loved so dearly, I felt comforted. Was it just a part of the cosmic nature that the rainbow appeared when and where it did? Perhaps. But I like to think it was a message that someday the two parts of the rainbow of my life will connect again in the distant sky.

As Thomas Pychon said in *Gravity's Rainbow*, "Death is a debt to nature due, which I have paid, and so must you." We can collect on that debt someday. One day when a rainbow comes stealing across the sky, we will fade with it. In the meantime, we can try to recall in our sorrow, as John Vance Cheney averred, "The soul would have no rainbow had the eyes no tears." Even in tears, we can clutch the portion of the rainbow that holds us to the earth, waiting for it to fade into the other end that waits someplace unseen.

In the middle of the most raging rainstorm

of my life, I will look for rainbows,

pausing to remember that rainbows take

both sunshine and rain.

Chapter 26

Dealing with the Finality of Death

O that 'twere possible,
After long grief and pain,
To find the arms of my true-love
Round me once again!
--Alfred Lord Tennyson

Death is so...final. A body once filled with life is now lifeless. It lies in a grave or in an urn, or even worse, maybe we don't even know or can't visit the final resting place of our loved one. No amount of wishing, no sea of tears or raging against the elements will bring our spouse back.

For the rest of our lives, we will awaken to the light of day without our cherished mate. The once blue sky is now gunmetal gray. All of the plans we had for our future evaporated with the last breath of the one with whom we hoped to share special times. The one with whom we thought we would grow old. The one we thought would be there to support us, to love us, and to care for us if needed. All that we had imagined gone with the last breath.

The hopes and dreams of future years together shattered, we are left alone, desolate, helpless to turn back the clock. Wishing won't help, regrets won't help, even praying won't bring back our loved one.

His life on earth is concluded. Done. Finished. The book of her life is closed, and while we may thumb through it nostalgically, treasuring the stories of the past, no more pages will be written. The conclusion can't be revised. No amendments, redrafts, modifications, or alterations are allowed. It sounds harsh. But it is indisputable.

In an effort to stay close to the physical body of our loved one, we visit her grave, laying flowers tenderly on the mound of clay that marks the place where the body now resides. If his body was cremated, we scatter the ashes, bury them, or keep the remains close to us.

At first, I carried my husband's urn to the den each morning when I arose, returning it to our bedroom each evening. Eventually, I began to leave it in the bedroom, but I still carry it whenever I go to our Florida condo—the place where we had dreamed of retiring together, spending our days looking out at the wide expanse of ocean and our evenings watching the sunset over the intra-coastal waterway. Bob's dream was to live there, and one of my biggest regrets is that the illness of one of his sheepdogs robbed him of that, despite my retirement to ensure it happened. So now it's just Bob's ashes, but I take them and sit them where they face the ocean. Silly, some may say. Senseless. A bit bizarre. Even weird. Perhaps it is all of those, but my inner being seems a little more peaceful when I do it.

Keeping Bob's urn close comforts me, but I know it does not change the finality of his death. He is still gone, and all I have left are his ashes. Nevertheless, it is the remains of what was once his physical body, and I cherish them. I know my way is not for everyone; each person has to deal with the remains of loved ones in whatever way brings a measure of consolation. No one, though, should ever be embarrassed for treasuring the vestiges of a life.

Arthur Schopenhauer tells us the deep pain we feel at the death of an individual "arises from the feeling that there is in every person something which is inexpressible, peculiar to him alone, and is, therefore, absolutely and irretrievably lost." Irreversible. Permanent. Final. So why should we be ashamed to hold on to whatever piece of the physical being that was? The spiritual being has moved on to another realm, and while we wait for a corporeal reunion of body and soul, we must each do what we can to get through the worldly finality of our loss.

An unknown author once wrote, "There are things that we don't want to happen but have to accept, things we don't want to know but have to learn, and people we can't live without but have to let go."

Sips of Sustenance

Letting go is hard, and holding on to the part that is left is okay if it helps us through the grieving process.

For a few moments each day, I will

remember my loved one's physical

presence, and in its absence, hold tight to

whatever I can to help me accept the

finality of loss.

Chapter 27

Accepting That Life Will Never Be the Same

Love is something eternal; the aspect may change, but not the essence.

--Vincent Van Gogh

If we trust Van Gogh's words, we still have the essence of our loved ones — it's just inside us rather than beside us. Footprints now fall on our hearts instead of solid ground. Yes, it's different. Undeniably, life will never be the same. And for a time, life may move in slow motion. John Dryden was right when he said, "Love reckons hours for months, and days for years; and every little absence is an age."

Without the anticipation of life together, we can sometimes be content to let life move as slowly as a freight train chugging up a steep mountainside. Without our spouse by our side, what reason do we have to move in a hurry, or to move at all?

It's tempting to stand still, to let the world continue to spin while we sit immobilized. We may not want to face life without our beloved. And if living forces us to do that, we may revolt, refusing to move forward. In rebellion, we may feel we don't have to live — even if we are still alive. Yet, to think that way diminishes the life we have been left. Each day is a gift, and accepting that life will never be the same doesn't mean we must condemn ourselves to a dreary existence.

Life is a matter of choices. We can choose to remain forlorn, lost, and dejected, or we can choose to be thankful for the life we shared with our loved one and move toward creating a life without him or her. Positive steps, even though they may be tiny ones, will move us in the right direction. We walk barefooted on spikes at first, but as Kenji Miyazawa advised, "We must embrace pain and burn it as fuel for our journey."

What, then, is required of us to accept life without our husband or wife? To plan for a future without her at its center? To envision a life without him?

The emotional part of facing life alone requires strength of will despite our sense that two hearts still beat as one. Nonetheless, instead of two souls thinking a single thought, we must now think alone. Emily Bronte pegged it when she said, "Whatever souls are made of, his and mine are the same." Disentangling our being is fraught with internal strife.

Perhaps we should just let emotions flounder — they will probably do that anyway — and address the more practical matters of life without our loved one. Do we want to stay in the same house? Do we want to move to another town? Do we have adequate financial resources to maintain our lifestyle? Do we want to go back to work?

Many advise that major life decisions should not be made for at least a year following a death, and that is probably sound counsel, but sometimes circumstances dictate otherwise. Even if we are not pressed to make critical choices, we should begin the thought process of envisioning our future. Living in limbo can take its toll, and having a plan or at least options can be an affirming step. After all, our loved one would not want us to stop living.

The road to a new life may be precipitous, and it may have detours, but it is a road we must travel. It's okay to be frightened and uncertain; it's not alright to stay stuck in a rut of self-pity. Dan Rather once wisely said, "Courage is being afraid but going on anyhow."

As difficult as it may be, for a few

moments each day, I will visualize my

future without my spouse. I will begin to

make plans for living, not just to exist. It's

what my beloved would want for me.

Chapter 28

Purging Yourself of Bitterness and Self-Pity

Growth in wisdom may be exactly measured by decrease in bitterness.

--Friedrich Nietzsche

When we are grief-stricken and bereft, bitterness runs down our throat like gall. We resent our loss. Sorrow sits heavy in our veins, and we want to blame someone or something—even God—for depriving us of our loved one. Righteous anger gives us a purpose, and the target is immaterial. Normally placid, we may become hostile toward the world and everyone in it.

Why was our spouse chosen and not someone else's? It's not fair. And so, we think, we have a right to be bitter, to feel sorry for ourselves. Such a reaction is not uncommon in the throes of sorrow, and we may like being cloaked by it. "Self-pity in its early stages is as snug as a feather mattress," Maya Angelou declared. But she quickly adds that when self-pity hardens, it becomes uncomfortable. In truth, losing a dearly loved companion is enough to justify self-pity for a while, but as Angelou says, if we stay in that stage of our grief too long, the hardness in our hearts creates a rough road through our sorrow.

There are people we never want to let go of, people we never want to see die. And it's tempting to think there has never been another love like ours. But when we look at the vast universe, when we look at the billions of people populating the earth, we comprehend that the one we lost was a speck in the sea of humanity — granted, a speck that captured our heart and made our world whole, but still like a grain of sand on a beach. Untold numbers of people have lived and died on this earth, and yet all we can see and feel at the moment is our one loss — the passing of an individual made in a unique mold, and thus absolutely and irretrievably lost.

That one loss fills us with bitterness and self-pity, and the only way to let go of these damaging emotions is to keep in mind that letting go isn't the end. What we had remains in our hearts; and what we lost, we hope to have again. We can choose to stay stuck in our sense of abandonment, or we can let go of what is already gone and, in Lao Tzu's words, become what we might be.

Helen Keller, whose life of blindness and deafness gave her reason for self-indulgence, believed that

Purging Yourself of Bitterness and Self-Pity

"Self-pity is our worst enemy and if we yield to it, we can never do anything wise in this world." Self-pity and bitterness can imprison us, holding us hostage from a life we might be able to lead. They ravage like cancer. If we can only release the thoughts that allow us to feel sorry for ourselves, we can escape the terminal condition of helplessness and frustration.

Robert Frost, whose poetry so often captures life at its essence, has this to offer: "In three words I can sum up everything I've learned about life: it goes on." Life goes on whether we stand still or travel with it. Surely there is something left for us in life, even without our beloved. If we are to find what awaits us, if we are to grow in wisdom, we must forsake our bitterness and self-pity.

I will believe, not just in my mind but in my heart, that others have suffered as much — and perhaps more — than I. With that thought, I will take a stab at setting aside my self-pity.

Chapter 29

Letting Go – Part 1

*You can clutch the past so tightly to your chest that it leaves
your arms too full to embrace the present.*

--Jan Glidewell

Pulling free of a loved one is akin to dislodging a
kite stuck in a tree. No matter how hard we tug, our
love is tangled in the limbs of our beloved. We are
stuck in the lyrics of the old song: "Letting go is hard
to do. My heart is filled with grief, I don't know what
to do, but every day I pray to God that I keep loving
you."

Candidly, we do not want to let go. We want to
keep loving our husband or wife, and in our stricken
minds, that means holding on. We righteously resist
any suggestion that we are holding on long after we
should have let go. We don't want to accept
separation. For some, it is as George Eliot whispered,
"Only in the agony of parting do we look into the
depths of love." Even if we recognized the intensity of
the love while our lives were entwined, now we see it
differently, sometimes through a rose-colored lens.

Perhaps these words from Old Yeller will help:
"That was rough...Thing to do now is try and forget

it...I guess I don't quite mean that. It's not a thing you can forget. Maybe not even a thing you want to forget. Life's like that sometimes...Now and then for no good reason a man can figure out, life will just haul off and knock him flat, slam him agin' the ground so hard it seems like all his insides is busted. But it's not all like that. A lot of it's mighty fine, and you can't afford to waste the good part frettin' about the bad. That makes it all bad...Sure, I know—sayin' it's one thing and feelin' it's another. But I'll tell you a trick that sometimes is a big help. When you start lookin' around for something good to take the place of the bad, as a general rule you can find it."

The hard part is finding the will to search for something to fill the void in our lives. We fear that would be betraying our spouse. That it would signal to others we didn't really love him or her as much as we said. But to think this way will allow our sorrow to sap the joy of our future. Seeking purpose and meaning in a life lived without our beloved is not being unfaithful. It is not disloyal. We owe it to ourselves to finish the journey of our own life. What loved one would want us to stop living before our heart stopped beating?

What, then, can fill the void? The answer is different for each person, but the possibilities are endless: become a Big Sister or Big Brother; visit the elderly or sick; help build a house with Habitat for Humanity; find a new hobby; develop new skills— take a class or get a friend to teach you something you've always wanted to learn; spend more time with family; travel; read for pleasure; garden; start a new business; volunteer with Hospice; or _____. You fill in the blank.

Nietzsche, a 19th century German philosopher, penned these words: "He who has a why to live can bear with almost any how." The needs of the world in which we live are great. Even in our grief, we can find a "why" to live for. Otherwise, we will find at the end, as Goethe predicted, "A useless life is an early death."

As hard as it will be, for a few moments today I will think about letting go — not of my memories — but of my grief. I will choose not to let sorrow be my constant companion and will occupy my mind and body with worthwhile activities.

Chapter 30

Letting Go – Part 2

We must be willing to let go of the life we have planned, so as to accept the life that is waiting for us.

--Joseph Conrad

Throughout our lives, we let go of possessions, people, events, and activities. Voluntarily or involuntarily we break apart from things and individuals with whom we have formed attachments —and sometimes it hurts. Perhaps never so badly as when the person who left was close to our heart. Unfortunately, occasionally we don't even know how much we care until the person is gone. Kahil Gibran was right when he said, "Love knows not its own depth until the hour of separation."

Despite new realization about the intensity of our affection and notwithstanding the extent of our pain, with death we have to let go. We can clutch memories, but we cannot hold the person we love. We can look at photographs, but we cannot see the person sitting next to us. Gone. Such a small word but it tears a hole in our hearts. It conjures up dreams and plans we had for our life together—dreams that will never be realized—plans that cannot be fulfilled.

Although we may not tell others, we have little desire to go on with life alone. We fear any life other than the one we had mapped out will be fruitless, unrewarding—maybe even frightening. Letting go of the past and the future we envisioned is tough, yet if we hold on to a plan now null and void, we will hit a roadblock that will forever detour us.

Until we are ready to let go, Havelock Ellis' wisdom may be a bridge between our past and our future: "All the art of living lies in a fine mingling of letting go and holding on." If we aren't ready to let go of our memories, we can still bait the line to fish in unknown waters. We don't know what we will catch, but at least the line has been cast.

None of us want to be like the birches in Robert Frost's poem, "bowed so low for long, they never right themselves." We don't want to let grief ride us like the young boy who rode the birch limbs down, "over and over again until he took the stiffness out of them." Rather, we want to be the narrator in "Birches," even when we are "weary of considerations, and life is too much like a pathless wood...," we only want to "get away from earth awhile and then come back to it and begin over." We don't want anyone to mistake our desire to stay with our sorrow for a wish to snatch us away, never to return.

No, even though we may climb the tree of grief toward heaven, "till the tree can bear no more," we want it to eventually dip its top and set us down again. Frost concludes his poem by writing, "One could do worse than be a swinger of birches." We, too, could have done worse. We could never have had the love we shared. Even though we are bowed down with ice that descended as a silent avalanche, we would never have given up the water that showered our soul with love just because it later turned to ice.

If you've ever seen the aftermath of an ice storm, you can picture the trees in "Birches." You can see the trees laden with ice, their faces turned toward the ground. While the ice remains, they do not try to straighten themselves, to be tall again. They understand their best chance of survival is to bend with the burden. As the ice slowly melts, their branches lighter, they again look toward the sun. Like trees, we must know when to bend, when to remain still, and when to stand up straight and strong again. If we try to rise too quickly, we, like trees, may break.

I will bend toward the ground with the ice

that covers me in my grief, but I will know

when to lift my shoulders, when to let the

sunshine melt my burden and draw my

eyes toward it again.

Chapter 31

Does Anyone Have a Nickel?

Now all night long Charlie rides through the tunnels saying, "What will become of me?"

--The MTA Song

An old song (written in 1949 by Jacqueline Steiner and Bess Lomax Hawes) tells of Charlie, a man who puts 10 cents in his pocket and heads out to board an MTA subway car, dropping his dime in the slot as he goes hurriedly through the turnstile. It seems the subway increased fares but didn't upgrade the machine that collected them, and Charlie doesn't know he needs an extra nickel until he tries to get off the subway. When the conductor tells him, "One more nickel," poor Charlie is stuck. Unable to come up with the nickel, he can't get off the train.

So Charlie rides the rails, stuck in the tunnels night and day. His wife brings him a sandwich every day and hands it to him through the window as "the train comes rumbling through." (I've never understood why she didn't just hand him a nickel!) The song's chorus is catchy and sticks in your mind:

"Did he ever return,

No he never returned

And his fate is still unlearn'd

He may ride forever

'neath the streets of Boston

He's the man who never returned."

Stuck in the tunnels of grieving, we may feel like Charlie. Unable to come up with the nickel to escape the darkness, get off the train, and return to life. Friends and family may offer us a sandwich when what we really need is a nickel. In other words, what they say may be well-intentioned, but it may not be what we need to "get off the train."

Trapped on the train of sorrow, how do we find a nickel? What seems a small sum to others is seemingly out of reach for us.

First, we have to determine what we need. Then, we have to be willing to work for the nickel. Maybe we have to sweep the floor of our souls to find the nickel. Or we may need to tell Charlie's wife [our family and friends] what is needed so they can discover a way to help—not just daily sustenance but an exit from the tunnels.

Some may find the comparison of sorrow to the MTA song ridiculous or even disrespectful. But there is a message if we are open to seeing it. Staying stuck in our past too long will keep us from grasping the future. "Out of a fear of the unknown," as Thich Nhat Hanh said, we "prefer suffering that is familiar."

Someone once remarked that getting over a painful experience is similar to crossing monkey bars. You have to let go at some point to move forward.

In the tunnel of my grief, I will look for a

way out. I know not what I may find, but I

will not let the uncertainty keep me

suffering, as familiar a zone

as that might be.

Chapter 32

Understanding the Void in Your Life

Where you used to be, there is a hole in the world, which I find
myself constantly walking around in the daytime, and falling in
at night. I miss you like hell.

--Edna St. Vincent Millay

As I sat writing today, I glanced out my kitchen window and saw dark, ominous clouds hanging low over the ocean. Turning to look out over the balcony behind me, I was shocked to see frothy white clouds with specks of blue sky peaking through. The contrast was startling—the two windows are only separated by a short span of wall, but the difference was disquieting. Looking one direction, the scene was gloomy and portentous; I turned my head and met an inviting view, full of sparkling sunshine.

The chasm between the two scenes represented the void in my life. I had fallen into the small space between the contrasting vistas. When my spouse was alive, our time together was like floating among the cumulous clouds in the azure sky. After his death, the storm clouds obscured the sunshine, and the windswept sea brought tears—sheaths of rain pouring down my face. Now, I float aimlessly between the two seascapes. No longer crying constantly but far from being ready to embrace the glare of sunlight again.

Why, I wonder, can I not climb out of the abyss into which I have fallen? The hole Edna St. Vincent Millay seemed to know so well? The hole countless others find themselves in when they lose a beloved companion?

Is it because the hole needs to be filled? Filled with what, I ponder? Long ago we had bonded like one body, one soul. Now the bond has been broken, leaving emptiness in its wake.

The old hymn says, "Once I was blind, but now I can see." To that tune I add new words, "Once I was whole, but now I am half." Part of me left and will never return. I can't even remember a time when we weren't together. I feel cut in two.

W.S. Merwin described his loss: "Your absence has gone through me like a thread through a needle. Everything I do is stitched with its color." The pattern taking shape in the tapestry of life with my loved one will now have to change. And the color of absence, as Merwin said, pervades the new design of my life.

When the night comes and the ocean is dark, I miss my mate. When the sun rises and brushes the waves, making them glisten, I miss him. When the noon sun sits high in the sky, warming the ocean breeze, I miss him.

Understanding the Void in Our Lives

As I rock on our front porch, gazing at the mountains in the distance, I yearn for him. As I walk through the garden of flowers we planted together, I pine for him. As I sit by the fireplace, watching the dancing flames, I wish he were sitting comfortably beside me.

Everywhere we are, everything we see, makes us long for our loved one. Memories burned so deeply into our mind every brain cell is indelibly branded.

Why did we not recognize the enormity of our love when our spouse was at our side? Is it human nature to fully recognize the extent of shared love only when our hearts are ripped out? When it is too late?

"How do I love thee? Let me count the ways. I love thee to the depth and breadth and height my soul can reach, when feeling out of sight for the ends of being and ideal grace." Words written more than a hundred years ago by Edna St. Vincent Millay, but words that quicken our spirits. Millay's famous poem tells how love stretches from our most quiet needs, how it fills the day from sunlight to candlelight. Purely and freely, Millay speaks of love with passion and concludes with these words: "I love thee with the breath, smiles, tears, of all my life! — and, if God choose, I shall but love thee better after death."

Can we fill the void created by love *with* love? Can we not continue to love even in physical absence? And cannot that love make us whole again? Merton says, "In all things there is a hidden wholeness." Perhaps we can find wholeness again by cherishing the love we had—and still have. If can heed the advice of P. J. Palmer, we will realize that "Wholeness does not mean perfection: it means embracing brokenness as an integral part of life."

Even in our brokenness, we can still find love to fill the void. It won't be the same, but it will be love and it can make us whole.

Understanding the Void in Our Lives

In the void in my heart I can still find love.

For a few moments each day, as I ache

from the hole inside me, I will be still and

let the warmth of the love we shared fill

me again.

Chapter 33

Love Never Ends

Love bears all things, believes all things, hopes all things, endures all things. Love never ends.

--I Corinthians 13: 7-8

Shared love cannot be snuffed out as a candle is extinguished by the wind. Rather, in the words of Francois Duc de la Rochefoucauld, absence increases great passion, a wind fanning a fire. If we were loved before the death of our beloved, that love can continue to grow within us. We can still be filled with that love.

No, the love will not be physical—we can no longer touch and hold our loved one. We can't share a warm embrace, a soft kiss, or an adoring look. But we can feel the love, remember the closeness, and recall the tender hugs. An old headstone in Ireland reads, "Death leaves a heartache no one can heal; love leaves a memory no one can steal." It is from those memories we can keep love alive.

Many years ago, my husband and I adopted a song, "The Twelfth of Never," as the theme song of our lives together. "You ask how long I'll love you, I'll tell you true—until the twelfth of never, I'll still be loving you." The night of his death, when I remembered a note in our safe that was marked, "To be opened after my death," I found he had signed it, "Until the twelfth of never, Bobby." And so, even after death, I know he still loves me, as I love him. We'll love each other, as the song goes, "'til the bluebells forget to bloom, 'til the clover has lost its perfume, 'til the poets run out of rhyme—until the twelfth of never, and that's a long, long time."

Sadly, one line in the song haunts me: "Hold me close; never let me go." Physical closeness is gone, but as I continue to live and grow, I can find new ways of feeling love and new paths for giving love. It would be a tragedy to stop loving because I can no longer hold my loved one in my arms.

Life is a game of cards. We may not like the hand we have been dealt, but if we want to stay in the game—if we want to live life—we must reshuffle the remaining cards and play. Love is stronger than death, and if we remain in the game, it can be an anesthetic for our pain.

Where can we look for this love? How can we keep it alive even in death?

Albert Ellis, a well-known psychotherapist, espoused that we choose what we think. We can make a conscious choice to think about love as present—not past. We can hold love fast, refusing to let it dissipate like a dying ember. Love made strong through living can survive death. We can persist in love, allowing our heart to stay open to it. We can look for love in memories, cherished notes, and special gifts. We can hold those in our hands and feel love emanating from them just as we did when our loved one was beside us. Isn't it worth the pain to have the memories?

Alfred Lord Tennyson held it true when he sorrowed most, "What ere befall, 'tis better to have loved and lost than never to have loved at all." At the darkest time of our grieving, we should never forget those words. We can see, even in our sorrow, that we have been blessed with a great love. We would never have given up the years of love just because we had to go through the agony of loss. The sting of sorrow smarts less with that realization. The greater our loss, the greater should be our gratefulness that we had so much to lose. It was a love worth living for—and now it is worth grieving over.

Erich Fromm, whose tragic love of Karen Horney was fulfilling even though it ended bitterly, shared this poignant reflection: "Who will tell whether one happy moment of love or the joy of breathing or walking on a bright morning and smelling the fresh air, is not worth all the suffering and effort which life implies."

Life is not all joy, and death is not all sorrow. Each has a balance, and we must find a way to steady the scale, accepting lows and highs on our own terms

165

while not letting it tip too far on the low side. In both life and death, love is both natural and irrational.

Love Never Ends

Today I will pause and cherish the love we
shared, looking through a telescope that
brings close what is now far. I will see a
distant canvas where love is reflected in
my soul.

Chapter 34

Saying Farewell

Parting is all we know of heaven and all we need to know of hell.

--Emily Dickinson

The dichotomy in Dickinson's words is heart-wrenching yet comforting. We certainly know the hell of parting from our spouse, and yet, it is from that same parting we hope and pray we know of heaven. We can choose to dwell on the thought of heaven or choose to live in the hell of our loss. The choice is ours. No one can make us let go and move on with our lives. And, truthfully, no one should try to force us on a set schedule. But sometimes we need a little nudge, and we should be thankful someone cares enough to give us a little push to get started on the rest of our lives.

Even though we are averse to saying goodbye, bidding our loved one adieu is part of getting through grieving. Words of farewell won't sever our bond, and we should not feel guilty when we get to the point where we can say, "Until we meet again."

An unknown author once asked, "Why does it take a minute to say hello and forever to say goodbye?" I think I know the answer — it's because the hello opens the portal to our relationship and we hurry to enter; saying goodbye seems as if we are closing the door on our beloved's life. If we can but see the closing of one gate as entry into another realm, we may be able to bear the send-off.

When and how do we say farewell? Like other parts of the grieving process, we must do it in a time and way in which we are most comfortable. Some do it orally — at a cemetery, standing on a mountaintop, or gazing at the ocean. Others do it symbolically, tenderly putting away visible reminders that keep sorrow flowing like sour wine. But we all have to do it. As much as we would like to, we can't pretend the person is coming back. We must accept the finality of the parting — at least on this earth.

Dust to dust, ashes to ashes. All that's left of our loved one's physical presence. The spirit of that person will always live in our heart, but the physical connections have taken their leave. Wouldn't it be wonderful if we could hold up a magnet and our loved one's magnet pulled him back to our side? But it is not to be. The body will turn to ash and dust, but our love isn't buried in the ground or scattered with the wind. We can still hold that close, though at some point, we must accept the parting and the time until we meet again. Love at its purest is not selfish, and in our heart we know our loved one wants us to let go and live again.

And, even after we say a fond farewell, we can remember that Richard Bach questioned whether miles (or a different dimension) truly separate us from our beloved. "If you want to be with someone you love, aren't you already there?"

Until we meet again, it will have to be enough to keep us going. As we say our farewell, perhaps we will hear our loved one giving us this old Irish blessing: "May the road rise up to meet you, may the wind be ever at your back. May the sun shine warm upon your face and the rain fall softly on your field. And until we meet again, may God hold you in the hollow of his hand."

As I bid adieu, I will be thankful goodbyes are not the end and they are not forever. They simply mean I will miss my loved one until we meet again.

Chapter 35

Life's Stage

All our yesterdays have lighted fools the way to dusty death. Out, out, brief candle! Life's but a walking shadow, a poor player that struts and frets his hour upon the stage and then is heard no more.

--William Shakespeare

All of life is a stage, and we are but shadowy characters who come on and off at the bidding of an unseen director. Our lives are but brief candles; they flicker for a moment in the eternity of time and then are snuffed out with the most unexpected whisper of wind. We strut and fret our time on the stage, and then the curtain closes on our life. The life we lived, according to Shakespeare, no more than a lighted path to a dusty grave.

Is Shakespeare trying to tell us, when he says, "and then is heard no more," that life ends with our last breath? If so, is all we do on this earth meaningless? Perhaps that's what Shakespeare surmises, since in Hamlet he avows, "The rest is silence."

Are we merely players, each with our own exits and entrances, as Shakespeare would have us believe? Is our exit the end not only for an earthly body but also the ethereal soul?

I hold no proof, but in a universe so magnificently designed, I believe our exit here is just the door to an entrance on another stage. Elizabeth Kubler-Ross, a world-renowned, Swiss-born psychiatrist who has written extensively on death and dying, would also have us believe that "Death is simply a shedding of the physical body like the butterfly shedding its cocoon. It is a transition to a higher state of consciousness where you continue to perceive, to understand, to laugh, and to be able to grow."

How can Kubler-Ross be sure? At the time she wrote the words, she had not crossed over to the other side so she had not been a first-hand witness. But, on the other hand, as Mahatma Gandhi said, "...we have no evidence whatsoever that the soul perishes with the body."

Life's Stage

In the absence of evidence to the contrary,

I can choose to believe that the departure

of my loved one on this stage of life was

not his final exit. For a few moments, I

will hold this thought close to my heart

today and be comforted.

Chapter 36

Why Aren't My Beliefs Strong Enough?

We tend to equate faith with a stoical attitude, not with tears.

--Granger Westberg

For a time, our faith may keep us strong. Maybe we even made it through the memorial service with our emotions so well in check people commented on our strength. But alone, seemingly ensconced in our home, grief may overwhelm us. Questions wiggle their way into our mind, and doubts confront us. When weeks—and perhaps months—pass and we still find ourselves engulfed with tears, we may begin to question our faith.

Whether overcome with tears or stoic in our silence, sorrow pervades our lives. Even in the midst of others, when we may submerge our feelings, inside us the pain flows.

For some the feeling is of great loss. For others, it is, as C.S. Lewis described, much like fear. "I am not afraid, but the sensation is like being afraid. The same fluttering in the stomach, the same restlessness, the yawning. I keep on swallowing."

And then, Lewis says, "At other times I feel mildly drunk, or concussed. There is a sort of invisible blanket between the world and me. I find it hard to take in what anyone says. Or perhaps, hard to want to take it in."

How can we feel this way if we believe in God? In Heaven? In life after death?

We go to God with our questions, and all we get is silence. We plead and beg for, if not answers, at least a "peace that passeth all understanding." If it doesn't come, we forlornly ask ourselves if our faith just isn't strong enough. Wouldn't God answer our prayers if we really believed? Would he, as C.S. Lewis described, just slam a door in our face and instead of an answer, we hear only "a sound of bolting and double bolting on the inside?"

Lewis, despite being adamant that we might as well turn away from the closed door, since "the longer we wait the more emphatic the silence will become," didn't think he was in danger of losing his faith—his belief in God. Instead, he declared, "The real danger is of coming to believe such dreadful things about Him. The conclusion I dread is not, 'So there's no God after all,' but 'So this is what God's really like. Deceive yourself no longer.'"

When we pray "Thy will be done," do we really mean it if God's will is that we lose a loved one? If it is his will, then why can't we find peace?

Why Aren't my Beliefs Strong Enough?

Are such questions heresy? If so, we join legions of others as heretics. The sacrilege, I think, is not in asking the questions but in thinking we would understand the answers even if they were given.

Each of us has to work our way through doubt and faith, and what satisfies others may not touch our need. I thus share how I worked my way to the other side with trepidation, knowing others may not arrive at the same conclusion.

First, after much praying, reading, and soul-searching, I have decided that I will never know all of the answers to my questions. I don't feel unfaithful for having asked them—God gave me a mind with which to think and reason—but my temporal state is on the other side of the door from where the answers reside.

Second, nature has shown me a master design for this world exists and is executed in cycles of birth and death. In such a seamless design, I cannot help but believe the creator has a plan for precious human beings after their life on this earth has been extinguished. While I may not see how the parts fit together in the puzzle of life and death, I can believe someone else does. I can believe that "All things work together for the good of them that love the Lord" even if I can't see the good from my earthly state.

I will not judge myself for lack of faith, realizing that being faithful doesn't mean not asking questions any more than being stoic doesn't mean I am not grieving.

Chapter 37

Jane Goodall on Life and Death

It was in the forest that I found "the peace that passeth understanding."

--Jane Goodall

Known for her pioneering work with chimpanzees, Jane Goodall saw humanity in ways most of us never envision. In her exploration of both science and soul, she found aspects of life and death that let her regain optimism even after her darkest hours.

In her book, *Reason for Hope*, Goodall says it was in the cathedral of Notre Dame in Paris that she came closest to experiencing the ecstasy of eternity as the silence surrounding the Rose Window exploded with an organ playing Bach's Toccata and Fugue in D Minor. The opening theme, she says, "seemed to enter and possess my whole self. It was as though the music itself was alive."

Caught up in the mystical music, Goodall's thoughts tumbled: "How could I believe it was the chance gyrations of bits of primeval dust that had led up to that moment in time—the cathedral soaring to the sky; the collective inspiration and faith of those who caused it to be built; the advent of Bach himself; the brain, his brain, that translated truth into music;

and the mind that could, as mine did then, comprehend the whole inexorable progression of evolution?"

Goodall could not believe it all was a matter of chance and so pronounced it "anti-chance." That meant she had to "believe in a guiding power in the universe—in other words, I must believe in God." Some may have difficulty reconciling Goodall's studies on evolution with her conviction that a supreme power had designed the world and all that is in it, but most can identify with her conclusion—that there is a God.

Nevertheless, Goodall almost lost her assurance that God exists when she watched her second husband lose an agonizing battle with cancer. It wasn't just the heartrending pain she witnessed that turned her from faith to rebellion, though. It was what we all feel when we lose a loved one—the finality of the loss. It's enough to make any of us waver.

Love, Goodall avows, takes many forms. We have love for friends, family, pets, country, nature, storms, the sea, and God. And like many, Goodall found that "The greater our love, the greater our corresponding sense of grief if the loved person or thing is lost." The deepness of our love determines the depth of our grieving.

Jane Goodall on Life and Death

For Goodall, the intensity of love for her husband was great. Intellectually, she had dealt with the concept of death many times, but the death of her dear husband Derek stung with a wildness she had never experienced before. She knew that invariably death follows life. She had seen the innate understanding of death not only in humans, but also in chimpanzees. She saw chimps learn from the death of one baby that the loss was irreversible. On the first death, a chimpanzee would continue to cradle the baby for three days—treating it as though it were alive until the dead body began to smell and attract flies. But when the same mother lost another child, although she still carried it for three days, it was without compassion—she dragged it by one leg, threw him over her back, dropped him headfirst to the ground. She knew it was hopeless to continue holding the dead child with care.

Goodall had heard stories from family members that led her to believe death was not a hopeless state. She recalls how her grandmother described the death of her own mother as she and a nurse sat together by her side: "'We both saw a silver wisp come out of her mouth, and hover for a moment, then vanish. We knew it was her soul leaving her body.'" Knowing of this experience, it hurt Goodall that she did not see her husband's soul depart, even though she sat beside him as he took his last labored breath. Her faith in God already bruised from watching her husband suffer, from having her prayers unanswered, she cried out in emotional exhaustion: "My God! My God! Why has thou forsaken me?" She questioned God and damned herself for failing to find a cure for her mate. She was angry at fate—at the unjustness of it all. And for a time, after her husband's death, she rejected God. But then she recalled the words she and her husband had spoken together so often during his illness, "As thy days, so shall thy strength be."

In her sorrow, her faith faltering, Goodall returned to the forest, hoping to find healing and strength. "Hoping that contact with the chimpanzees, so accepting of what life brings them, would ease my grief."

She knew that "In the forest, death is not hidden— or only accidentally, by the fallen leaves. It is all around you all the time, a part of the endless cycle of life. Chimpanzees are born, they grow older, they get sick, and they die. And always there are the young ones to carry on the life of the species." Goodall continues, "These things brought a sense of perspective back into my life, and with it peace. Gradually, my sense of loss was purged of bitterness, and the futile railing against fate was stilled."

It didn't happen quickly. At first, as she returned to her home in the forest, where she had known such happiness with her Derek, she was desperately sad. Her house "peopled, now, by ghosts." And then, one night something extraordinary happened. Lying in the bed they had shared, "listening to the sound of the waves on the shore, the crickets, all the familiar night sounds," she heard Derek speak to her. It seemed that he spoke for a long time, telling her important things, things she should know, things she should do. Was she awake? She doesn't know. She just knows Derek was there. "And even as he spoke, my body, all at once, went rigid, and the blood rushed and pounded in my ears. Roaring, roaring." And when it stopped, Goodall remembered nothing at all —only that her husband had been there and that he had had a joyful message for her. "Nothing more. None of the wisdom."

Goodall knew what happened had not been a normal dream. She awoke utterly exhausted but "happier, more able to cope." What occurred reinforced truth she had always known: "...mind can communicate with mind across time." Acknowledging that science demands objective factual evidence, in other words, proof, Goodall admits spiritual experiences are subjective and can only be accepted by faith. For her, it was enough that her faith gave her an inner peace and brought meaning to her own life.

During the first six months or so after her husband's death, Goodall often felt his presence. "I had a strong conviction that in his spirit state he could not see or hear — or perhaps it was that he could not feel the things he had loved in earthly life — the sea, the pounding waves, ballet, the graceful hand-over-hand swinging of the young chimpanzees playing in the trees." But Goodall felt passionately that if she looked and listened with great attention, Derek would be able to enjoy them through her eyes and ears. And then, she says, "After a while, as though he knew that I was all right, that my days had, indeed, brought sufficient strength, I felt his presence less and less often. I knew it was time for him to move on and I did not try to call him back."

I know my experiences will not mirror
those of others, but I will draw strength
from them as I make my way through my
own wilderness. The sum of all the myriad
contacts others — and perhaps I — have had
with deceased loved ones will sustain my
belief in life after death.

Chapter 38

What Happens After Death?

When I lay my questions before God I get no answer. But a
special sort of No answer. It is not the locked door. It is more like
a silent, certainly not uncompassionate, gaze. As though He
shook his head not in refusal but in waiving the question. Like
"Peace, child. You don't understand."

--C.S. Lewis

Having grown up in a Christian home, the concept of life after death was one I never questioned. When my parents died from terminal illnesses, many years apart, I grieved, but my faith, combined with relief they were no longer suffering, helped me through the mourning process. Biblical verses like, "This day thou shalt be with me in paradise," and "If I go to prepare a place for you, surely I will come again," comforted me. Sitting in church, hearing the choir sing songs of heaven such as "In the Sweet By and By," "Shall We Gather at the River," "When We All Get to Heaven," and "I'll Fly Away," my heart would swell with anticipation of a glorious reunion. I was particularly heartened by the belief that heaven was guaranteed for anyone just by asking for forgiveness.

When my husband of 37 years died, my whole belief system almost crashed. Simple scriptures no longer sufficed. I wanted concrete answers. And what appeared to be contradictions in scripture troubled me, making me question previously accepted concepts.

Where is this place called heaven? Above us, we see the "heavens" on sunny days and in starlit lights. We see them covered with fat, cumulous clouds or unfurling their fury with laser-like shooting streaks of lightning and crashing claps of thunder. Is this where God resides? Is this where we will spend eternity? Likely not, at least not the parts of the heavens man has explored in his space travels, as immense and glorious as they are. We must suffice it to say that God's abode—and our future home—will be higher and grander than anything we have ever seen or imagined. As described in Isaiah 65:17 and II Peter 3:13, we will see new heavens.

But more questions follow.

If the day a person dies he or she will be in paradise, then why does the scripture also declare, "The dead in Christ shall rise" on the day of final judgment. Does a person's soul go to heaven as soon as the last breath is drawn, or does it exist in some kind of never, never land until the body is resurrected? As Mason Cooley whispered, "Eternity eludes us, even as a thought."

In this illusion of eternity, we must ask the question, what is the soul? Both ecclesiastic scholars and simple believers have described it in a host of ways. To some, "soul" and "spirit" are synonymous. To others, they are two separate but linked entities. In the end, while I decided I agreed with Mary Oliver when she said, "Nobody knows what the soul is. It comes and goes like the wind over the water," I also believe that—whatever it is—the soul is the part of humanity that connects human beings to God.

Despite innumerable questions with no certain answers, I am not able to shake my belief in an afterlife. We came to this world from a place unknown. Yes, we know that, literally, we came from an egg and a sperm, but where life began is a mystery, even if some believe they know "how." Whether it began as a big bang and slowly evolved or was created in seven days, I agree with Goodall that a master plan was in progress, which means a master designer must exist.

Ralph Waldo Emerson described our entrance and exit into life this way: "Out of sleep a waking. Out of waking a sleep." I would add a third line: "Awake again from sleep—a final time." We come from a womb and go to a tomb. Both can be described with accuracy. The third resting place has yet to be portrayed with any certainty.

Walter Scott asked the question, "Is death the last sleep?" and answered it by saying, "No, it is the last final awakening." What we shall see when we escape remains a mystery. The more I study, the more confused I become. I'm reminded of words written by T.S. Eliot: "What we call the beginning is often the end. To make an end is to make a beginning. The end is where we start from."

Like Herman Melville, I know that "Hope is the struggle of the soul, breaking loose from what is perishable, and attesting her eternity." In the master plan of the universe—whose existence I have never doubted—I have to believe eternity is more than Thomas Moore described: "From my rotting body, flowers shall grow and I am in them and that is eternity."

Tulips come back as tulips; jonquils as jonquils, irises as irises. I refuse to believe the departed will come back only as a flower. Rather, I will choose to adopt the wisdom of Kahlil Gibran: "I existed from all eternity and, behold, I am here; and I shall exist till the end of time, for my being has no end."

What form that "being" takes is more than I can contemplate or imagine, but the alternative, believing life ends when the last breath is drawn, is less than I will accept. I must be content to believe, as Solomon did, that "The souls of the righteous are in the hands of God."

And the end of all our exploring
Will be to arrive where we started. . .
--T.S. Eliot

As I struggle with grief, I will allow

myself to question my beliefs, knowing

they can withstand the examination if they

are true. What I cannot discern in human

terms, I will accept with hope and faith,

content to know that someday I will

understand.

Chapter 39

The Kaleidoscope Turns

*...the alteration of all life's schemes and all its scope...all with
one tiny turn of life's kaleidoscope.*

--Danielle Steel

The many prisms of our lives turn as mirrors and colored shapes inside a kaleidoscope. As the patterns shift, the hues and complexities of the parts of our lives blend and separate, only to re-form in new configurations—sometimes bright and splendid; sometimes dark and cheerless.

When an unseen hand twists the kaleidoscope, as in the death of a spouse, the patterns of our life shift outside our control. Paraphrasing Steel's poem, the spectrum swings from bright to dark, from grand to grim, and from joy to sorrow, as we stand by helplessly, watching the changes reshape our lives in ways we had not planned. The alteration of scenes we had envisioned for the coming years—all with one tiny twirl of life's kaleidoscope. The pieces have now fallen into a different design.

If you've ever held a kaleidoscope in your hands, you know each turn brings a different kind of beauty —uncommon patterns, distinctive colors, singular splendor. Each twist wipes out the present exquisite view and replaces it with another, just as magnificent.

Sips of Sustenance

Is it possible, then, to turn the colors of death in the kaleidoscope into a more peaceful pattern — colors perhaps softer than before but not bleak and shadowy?

An unseen hand may have twisted the kaleidoscope into a dark death tomb, but our hands can twist the end whenever we are ready to design a new scene. Elizabeth Kubler-Ross admonished if we shield canyons from windstorms, we will never see the true beauty of their carvings. And if we fail to turn the kaleidoscope, we may never see the splendor that lies ahead in our lives. If we are always waiting, in Steele's words, for "tomorrow and a twist of fate," the kaleidoscope view stands still, immobilized by its scene of sorrow. If, however, we choose to seek a ray of hope, Steele says it only takes the faintest slight of hand to alter what we see in life.

In Steele's poem, we learn we can move from the gentle twist that brought the darkest night to "happy rhymes and gentle songs." Yes, we must go "from the brightest dawn to deepest dusk, from morning sun to twilight dreams," and we must face "lives that sometimes go awry." From "shining hopes" of the past, we must deal with "sudden turns" that reshape our future. But we can choose to grasp hold of the end of the kaleidoscope and twist again. Thankfully, the hand that turned the kaleidoscope toward death has let go for now, and the next twist is in our hands.

The Kaleidoscope Turns

For a few moments today, I will turn the
kaleidoscope, allowing new prisms of
light and hope to push aside the gloom
and sadness coloring my world.

Chapter 40

You Don't Have to Feel Guilty If You Are Happy

Birds sing after a storm; why shouldn't people feel as free to delight in whatever remains to them?

--Rose Kennedy

If anyone ever had cause to succumb to life's tragedies, Rose Kennedy did. The matriarch of the Kennedy family lost child after child, more than any mother should ever have to bear. For her, sorrows came, in Shakespeare's words, "not as single spies but in battalions." And yet she bore the losses not only with dignity and grace, but also with a heart that nevertheless found joy in life. That we all could emulate her peaceful spirit...

The temptation is to shield ourselves from happiness, to shy away from joy. Sometimes we don't want to be removed from our sorrow because we fear guilt will come with happiness. How can we enjoy life again when our loved one can no longer experience earthly joys? Don't we owe it to him to be sad? Would we not betray her love if we let go of our sorrow?

Cicero said, "There is something pleasurable in calm remembrance of a past sorrow." The key word is "past." To get to the pleasurable part of remembrance, we have to put the sorrow in the past. And Cicero believed that "There is no grief that does not lessen and soften." The old platitude that time will help in more elegant words. Turning to common vernacular, Cicero admonished, "It is foolish to tear one's hair in grief, as though sorrow would be made less by baldness."

Did Cicero think we *want* to grieve? Most pray to be delivered from mourning. Even when we try, escaping is not easy. Keats said when he "bade sorrow good-morrow and thought to leave her far away behind," she [sorrow] loved him so dearly she followed him constantly.

How, then, do we leave the storm of sorrow behind? How do we find the rainbow it paints in its wake?

First, we must admit we will miss the tears when the eventual easing of grief comes, as Mahfooz Ali avers. Ali reminds us we will not likely be eager to begin the dance of life again without our loved one, "for the world has lost its wonder for [us], some of its shine...." But somewhere, sometime, we will once again feel free to love life, even though we know we may lose again.

When we see a faint rainbow in the sky of our life, we should follow it. To find its pot of gold, we may have to willingly suspend our disbelief that we can ever be happy again. The artist's palette has the glorious colors needed; we just have to pick up the brush and paint the strokes. Life begins on the other side of that rainbow, on the other side of our sorrow, with or without the gold. If within us there is still a love of life, Benjamin Franklin warned that we should not squander time, for that is what life is made of.

What does it take from us to love life again?

Someone to care about.

Something to hope for.

Something to do (a purpose).

The first part of the trilogy is easy. The world is full of people needing our love, our caring concern. They can be found in nursing homes, in hospitals, under bridges, in orphanages, around our neighborhoods — perhaps even in our own homes — and countless other places. The second part is a little harder; if we keep it simple — hoping for peace in the midst of our storm — we can surely crawl to the tip of the branch on the wings of hope and begin the slow flight back to hopefulness. The final item, purpose, leads us back to the first — love. Disraeli once wisely stated that "We are born for love; it is the principle of existence and its only end."

Love brought us to our knees with its loss. It can pick us up again and put us firmly on our feet if we will open our hearts to share the love, like lighting candles, one passing its glow to the next, in the darkness of our lives.

In my bleakest moments, I may not want to seek happiness, but I may find it if I share the love I gave to my beloved with others. It may bring me joy, and my loved one will rejoice.

Chapter 41

Finding a New Sense of Purpose

Sometimes in tragedy we find our life's purpose – the eye sheds a tear to find its focus.

--Robert Brault

For 37 years one of the primary purposes of my life was to love and care for my husband. His death stripped me of that closely held work; and, because I had retired just eight months before he died, I had already left behind my self-fulfilling goals as a university president. Two significant changes occurred in my life in less than a year. One made by choice with eager anticipation of years together at our oceanfront condo, gazing sleepily at a coppery sunrise, watching grey storm clouds build over the horizon, and walking hand in hand on the sand. The other choice fell on my head without my input or concurrence – my husband was gone in an instant, and I was left without a reason to exist. The life we had planned together evaporated with his last breath. We had hoped, as Robert Browning avowed, to grow old together, because "the best [was] yet to be."

Whether our sense of being is tied to our loved one's existence, its absence surely takes away part of who we are and what we do. In our attempt to hold onto the life we shared, we must be cautious we don't forego the present.

Even if we let go of the past, one of the dangers we face after the death of a person central to our life is the temptation to jump from the present to the future without living in the here-and-now. We can bear to think about years ahead because they are distant, but today our loss is so unbearable we want to escape. The future may be uncertain, but the present is untenable. For months, we wake each day and the absence of our spouse is palatable. Getting through a day is hard enough; trying to find a purpose for existence is more than we can tackle.

What we can do is take a few moments each day to concentrate on what's important in life. Even in our grief, we can find ways to be kind to others; to be generous and loving. We may not be able to devise a master plan for the week, or even the day, but we can focus on one person for a few moments. Beyond that, we may simply find purpose in appreciating nature — a newly awakened bulb, a landscape ablaze with color, a mountain range capped with angel hair. Or, we can pause momentarily to watch a child playing in the rain, a dog romping in the park with its master, a butterfly breaking free of its cocoon. After all, isn't the appreciation of life a purpose in and of itself?

However man arrives on this planet, he was given eyes to see and ears to hear the wonders of this world. Notwithstanding the chasm of loss, we can see hope in a star and hear the brush of leaves blowing in the wind. What greater purpose do we have than to experience the simplicity and complexity of an earth so grand the human mind cannot fathom its full scope?

Each piece of the universe matters somehow. We may not know the scheme — cannot see the grand plan — but surely there is a purpose to all things in life and death. It is in that pattern our purpose will be found if we are open to a new picture. If Robert Byrne was right, that "The purpose of life is a life of purpose," we must draw our life on a new canvas, using a different palette. Sadness may fly on the wings of our discovery of fresh meaning in our lives.

George Santayana said, 'There is no cure for birth and death, save to enjoy the interval." If we can, let's take pleasure in life. Let us heed the words penned by an unknown writer: "Life is not about waiting for the storms to pass ... it's about learning how to dance in the rain."

I will not wait until I can see the future clearly before I embrace the present. In small ways, for brief moments, I will re-engage in the life about me, finding purpose serendipitously.

Chapter 42

All Shall Be Well

All shall be well, and all shall be well and all manner of thing shall be well.

--Julian of Norwich

Can it be? Can it really be that all shall someday be well again in our lives? We have to believe it is so, or we will literally go crazy. At first, when we are beset with tears, unable to sleep at night, we have hope we will feel better in a few days or weeks. But then, months pass, and while our tears may not flow unchecked, the intensity of our grief remains. Filling the gaps in our tears is a sense of aloneness, a despair that our husband or wife is no longer at our side, a feeling that where we were whole, now we are broken.

Alfred Lord Tennyson captured the thoughts of many when he wrote, "Gone—flitted away, taken the stars from the night and the sun from the day! Gone, and a cloud in my heart."

No more sunshine and no more stars. We are tempted to feel as William Cowper did: "Absence from whom we love is worse than death, and frustrates hope more severe than despair."

Can hope be restored? Can all manner of things be well? These questions can be answered in only three ways: "No, I have no hope." "Yes, I have hope." And for those with strong religious beliefs, "I know all shall be well again." Each person must choose one of these responses. In many ways, it is not difficult to at least choose between the first two possibilities. To admit we have no hope that all will be well condemns us to a life of despair. Who would voluntarily choose that fate? Even in our lowest moments, we need to find a morsel of hope to sustain us until we can see the sun and stars again. Our anticipation of a better life may be only a crumb, but we need to devour it as a starving person, giving us enough sustenance to make it through another day. Scrap by scrap, the food of hope can give us energy to re-grow our interest in life.

From whence does hope come? For many, it derives from a belief that the person we loved did not die when the body became cold. If we can believe, as William Penn did, that "...death is no more than a turning of us over from time to eternity," we can draw comfort and find hope that our husband or wife continues to live in another dimension.

With the hope of a reunion, the expectation that our remaining time on earth can be lived with a sense of peace and contentment should be our goal. The scriptures promise a "peace that passeth understanding." In our darkest hours, we think to have peace again would indeed take a miracle that we will never understand.

No living person can describe in definitive detail what eternity is like, and that inability to understand sometimes makes us question if there is life after death. If we wait for proof, we will spend the rest of our lives in misery. If we have the faith of a mustard seed, our belief can grow mightily if we nourish it.

It is important to remember that just as there is no tangible proof of life beyond death, there is also no scientific evidence supporting a contention that life ends with our last breath. Since neither proof nor disproof exists, why not choose to believe and be comforted, knowing that for our beloved spouse all is now well and for us, all shall be well.

Then, and only then can we accept Shakespeare's prophetic statement, "God knows when we shall meet again."

The following words were spoken at a sermon by Henry Scott Holland, Canon of St. Paul's Cathedral in London, following the death of King Edward VII. Although many scholars question the contradictions between these thoughts and others expounded by Holland throughout his life, they poignantly describe what we all hope to be true of life and death.

Sips of Sustenance

"Death is nothing at all, I have only slipped away into the next room. I am I and you are you; whatever we were to each other, that we still are.

Call me by my old familiar name. Speak to me in the easy way you always used. Put no difference in your tone. Wear no forced air of solemnity or sorrow. Laugh as we always laughed at the little jokes we shared together. Let my name ever be the household word that it always was. Let it be spoken without effect, without the trace of a shadow on it.

Life means all that it ever meant. It is the same as it was; there is unbroken continuity. Why should I be out of mind because I am out of sight? I am waiting for you, for an interval, somewhere very near, just around the corner.

All is well.

Nothing is past; nothing is lost. One brief moment and all will be as it was before.

How we shall laugh at the trouble of parting when we meet again!"

All Shall be Well

In my confusion, I will choose hope over
despair, believing that someday, from
another dimension, I will look back and
see the time apart was short. With that
conviction, all shall be well.

Sherry L. Hoppe, Ed.D.

Sherry Hoppe is the primary author of *A Matter of Conscience, Redemption of a hometown hero, Bobby Hoppe*, as well as authoring and editing books on higher education for the academic market.

Dr. Hoppe's first career was as a counselor before getting her Ed.D in higher education and entering the academic world. She is the retired president of Austin Peay State University and served as president at Roane State College and Nashville State College.